I0221409

Quarterly Essay

Quarterly Essay is published four times a year by Black Inc., an imprint of Schwartz Books Pty Ltd. Publisher: Morry Schwartz.

ISBN 9781863954440 ISSN 1832-0953

Subscriptions – 1 year print & digital
(4 issues): $79.95 within Australia incl. GST.
Outside Australia $119.95. 2 years print & digital
(8 issues): $149.95 within Australia incl. GST.
1 year digital only: $49.95.

Payment may be made by Mastercard or Visa, or by cheque made out to Schwartz Books. Payment includes postage and handling.

To subscribe, fill out and post the subscription card or form inside this issue, or subscribe online:

quarterlyessay.com
subscribe@blackincbooks.com
Phone: 61 3 9486 0288

Correspondence should be addressed to:

The Editor, Quarterly Essay
22-24 Northumberland Street
Collingwood VIC 3066 Australia
Phone: 61 3 9486 0288 / Fax: 61 3 9011 6106
Email: quarterlyessay@blackincbooks.com

Editor: Chris Feik
Management: Sophy Williams, Caitlin Yates
Publicity: Elisabeth Young
Design: Guy Mirabella
Production Co-ordinator: Adam Shaw

THE HISTORY QUESTION

Who Owns the Past?

Inga Clendinnen

The "history wars" might be over, but history is in the news again because the Prime Minister has put it there. The putsch began in mid-2004 with the announcement of a $31 billion education package from the federal government. Certain conditions had to be met before schools would get their bonus funding, among them that "every school must have a functioning flagpole, fly the Australian flag and display a 'values framework' in a prominent place in the school." The Prime Minister, John Howard, and the then Education Minister, Brendan Nelson, assured us that "this is a major investment in Australia's future … It will leave us better equipped to face the global future and help us build on our long traditions of innovation and technical excellence." That seems a lot of hope to invest in a piece of fabric and a poster, but if the connection was obscure, the intention was plain.

Then came the Prime Minister's 2006 Australia Day speech. Only a couple of paragraphs related to the nation's history, but they were heartfelt, so we would be wise to pay attention.

Mr Howard is concerned about the state of the teaching of history, especially Australian history, in schools today. There is too little of it, too few students are studying it, it is the wrong kind of history anyway: "Too often it is taught without any sense of structured narrative, replaced by a fragmented stew of themes and issues. And too often history, along with other subjects in the humanities, has succumbed to a postmodern culture of relativism where any objective record of achievement is questioned or repudiated."

Mr Howard wants a "structured narrative", and he wants that narrative to be an "objective record of achievement" which will make us proud of our country, our forebears and ourselves. History fuses easily with patriotism; Mr Howard wants them fused: "We want [newcomers] to learn about our heritage. And we expect each unique individual who joins our national journey to enrich it with their loyalty and their patriotism." It is to achieve those ends that he wants "a root and branch renewal of the teaching of Australian history in our schools".

I had become accustomed to listening to my Prime Minister with a degree of nervous dread, so I was surprised to find myself in sympathy with much of his speech, even with his longing for a clear, celebratory story of how Australia got to be the fine country it undoubtedly is. I think he wants his story because he thinks we're going to need it. For most of our immigration history we have managed to avoid significant ethnic or religious clotting, with most incomers dispersing throughout the country within a generation. Now there is the risk of the geographical concentration and the social isolation of people of a different and charismatic faith who share a long and continuing history of injustice at European hands, and this at a time of decreasing job security and shrinking opportunities. Furthermore, with intolerant religions and amoral global capitalism snatching more and more territory in the world, secular liberal democracies begin to look less like the highway to the future and more like an endangered species. But despite my sympathy, I think it will be difficult for Mr Howard to arrive at his "objective record of achievement", and then to present it as "Australian history", for a number of reasons.

The first is that in human affairs there is never a single narrative. There is always one counter-story, and usually several, and in a democracy you will probably get to hear them. Remember the origin of the history wars. A lot of Australians wanted to go on telling themselves the stories their fathers had told them about the triumph of British explorers and settlers in overcoming this recalcitrant land: about smoke rising from slab huts, the sound of axes ringing through the blue air, and so on. They were good stories; they sometimes approximated what happened; they also made people feel good. Then along came this fellow named Henry Reynolds who said, "Hold it. There's another story going on here. These other things happened too, and I can prove it." As he proceeded to do. Consternation. But now, except for the die-hards, there is (sometimes grudging) acceptance that yes, there is another story interwoven with our own, a story about what happened to the people who were here before the British came, and attention must be paid to that story, too.

If you (or Mr Howard) are still yearning for a single, simple story without historians spoiling your fun, consider the ditty which ought to be our national anthem instead of the dingo-wail we have now: *Waltzing Matilda*. The plot is straightforward. A swagman is settling down by a billabong after a hard day's swagging. A jumbuck comes down to drink at the billabong, the swagman grabs him, stuffs him into his tuckerbag. So there he is, sitting in the shade of a coolibah tree, his billy is boiling, soon he will be having a free mutton dinner. Peace. Happiness. Then his home-made Eden is disrupted: up comes the squatter mounted on his thoroughbred, up come the troopers one two three, the squatter challenges him – "Whose is that jumbuck …?" – and the swagman declares his contempt for such footling concerns by jumping out of the frying pan and into the billabong, which he now haunts in a posthumous claim to rightful possession.

That is the story from the swagman's point of view. What values does it celebrate? Death before submission, especially submission to corrupt authority. Property is theft. Troopers are the running dogs of pastoral capitalism. (You can see why Howard favours *Advance Australia Fair*.) Switch to the squatter, and the values change. He knows the time, the sweat and the money it took to get his merinos to this good place, and now here is this useless layabout stealing one. (Some of the blackfellas around the place used to do that too. He soon cured them.)

As for the troopers: they might have thought the swagman was a useless layabout; they might have envied his freedom; they might have been looking forward to their own stolen mutton dinner. They might have felt any of those things, or none of them, or something quite different. They don't speak, they don't act. We only know their official role. We have no clue as to what was in their hearts. By contrast, I think the jumbuck would have had a view about hairless lamb-murdering hypocrites who pretend to have your interests at heart – "Please, have this grass, have this water, watch out for that dingo!" – and then turn on you. I doubt the jumbuck saw much difference between the humans, whether swaggie, squatter or trooper, or their equine companions either.

If you are a good historian (the fine thing about history is that you don't have to be a professional to do it well), you will already have noticed that this is a place of shade and good water: that there would have been other camp-fires here. You might also have noticed those rippling syllables of "billabong", "coolibah". What might the coolibah tree be thinking? That this strange breed of biped with their sharp-hoofed companions are squabbling over meat where once there had been soft-footed people who moved lightly over the land; who fought, but not over meat. This four-verse, sixteen-line song turns out to be more complicated than it looked. And the layers of stories don't end there: if we kept burrowing under that coolibah tree we would come to Gondwanaland and tectonic plates, which thankfully lie beyond historians' jurisdiction.

If you were a practising historian, you would also want to know where the song came from: who had made it out of what experience for what purpose. *Waltzing Matilda* was invented by a man called Paterson, self-named "Banjo", in 1895. Banjo Paterson was no swagman. He was no bushman, either, having left his family's farm for Sydney Grammar School when he was ten. He was a city-based lawyer and a sometime poet who published in the ardently nationalistic *Bulletin*, and he did a great deal to create the myth of the tough men created by the tough Australian bush. He wrote *Matilda* four years after the bitter shearers' strike. Squatters were not popular then, or not among the readers of the *Bulletin*. Paterson constructed his swagman saga out of the hard politics of the early 1890s.

If *Matilda* was in its beginnings a political work, how far was Paterson being "historical"? Was his swagman representative of the men who tramped Australian roads in late nineteenth-century Australia? The closest I have come to a "real" swagman on-the-page was years ago, when John Hirst was editor of *Historical Studies* and inveigled me both into print and into Australian history by asking me to review a book called *The Diary of a Welsh Swagman*. Joseph Jenkins was nothing like my old friend in the billabong. He was a sober-minded ex-farmer who tramped the roads to find a halfway well-run farm where he could work and not have to watch animals and machinery ruined through pure neglect. He sang not in billabongs, but at eisteddfods, and won prizes, too. He was no vagabond, but a solid citizen who wrote letters to the newspapers denouncing the poor husbandry he saw all around him. Was he "typical"? No. A lot of men humped their swags through rural Australia, hard workers most of them, and some of them supported families. Some were lawless. Some were not. Tramping was how people got about, unless (like squatters, like troopers) they kept a horse.

Nowadays we take *Waltzing Matilda* easily, enjoying its extravagances along with our mild contempt for outsiders who don't know what "jumbuck" and "billabong" and "waltzing Matilda" mean. We like the tune. We like the sentiment, too, however fast it is eroding. That might be why we like it — because it is a relic from a remote past. Or is it important to us not because it is a fragment of history, but because it is not: an invented moment masquerading as an icon of a fictional all-white past?

Whatever its origins and status, now it sits, comfortable, unexamined, in the contemporary collective consciousness. But some of us have longer memories. I remember swagmen from the years just before the Second World War. My mother was frightened of strangers, but she was not afraid of the quiet, unshaven men who sometimes knocked on our kitchen door. My mother was a frugal woman, but she was not frugal with them: she would sit them down on the back step and set about making them huge meat sandwiches and a big pot of tea. They would sit on the step, drink their tea and eat their sandwiches while she made up another batch for the road, slipping in a handful of her best shortbread. Then they would thank her (they called her "Missus"), hoist their bundles and go. I would watch them walk away down the road at an oddly slow, steady pace, and think, "Where can they be going?", but if I asked my mother she would purse her lips, shake her head and turn away.

That was in the late '30s. Why were there men on the road then? Why were they so silent? Now I think it was the silence of humiliation: other women along the street would screech at swaggies and order them away, muttering about their chooks. Why did my mother invite them in and feed them so eagerly? Now I think she was remembering her own child-hood, with her father's lungs ruined by coal dust and her mother ped-dling scones in the Port Melbourne street to feed her six children. My mother had been through the Great Depression, too. She knew what it was to be down on your luck.

I seem to have absorbed her attitudes. For me, these "swagmen" were never jolly fellows emancipated by an act of will from the constrictions of their class, but rather embodiments of the human costs of the system which was keeping the rest of us warm and secure. I always enjoyed the defiance of Paterson's swaggie before the complacent authority of the squatter, but it is only now, looking back, that I see how from early on I transformed his fictional swagman into a working-class warrior.

Nowadays the bush myth is alive and serving present purposes well, although now the squatter has the central role, as when The Men from Snowy River clatter up Collins Street in their R.M. Williams outfits in defence of their inalienable right to graze their cattle on public land, or the Prime Minster dons his Akubra, Pastoralist Style, to signify his solid worth. Meanwhile the billabong swagman has become an innocuous icon of feckless freedom. But the resonances of the idea remain specific to us. When I was living in the United States with two small boys, I suddenly had to concoct costumes for an impromptu fancy-dress party. So I dressed them as swaggies. On the way out we met the African-American janitor, who had become a friend. He shook his head incredulously and said, "You're sending them as *bums*?" and I realised how parochial I had been in my iconography. Australian swaggies are not American bums. But how to explain the difference?

Here I have tried to show how the root-system of an invented but vital myth can bind a person to the nation and to the national culture, while remaining sufficiently flexible to allow any number of individual emphases and uses, including cynical ones. A successful myth only grows more potent with exploitation. Down at the beachfront there is a shop selling mainly to tourists and backpackers. Yesterday a toy was on special display: a koala wearing a leather waistcoat and a slouch hat, waving a bunch of green plastic gum leaves. If you poked a button hidden under his waistcoat, his stomach would croak a verse of *Waltzing Matilda*. The shopkeeper misread my interest and said, "Awful, isn't it? Made in China!" It was both awful and made in China. But I still wanted it.

"Waltzing Matilda" has become a durable myth, commanding general recognition and affection yet remaining sufficiently capacious to contain a jumble of personal associations. Its expansiveness is the problem. Mr Howard's ambition is to extend the scope of the values he sees as common to old Australia to embrace newcomers. He specifies these common values as "respect for the freedom and dignity of the individual, a commitment to the rule of law, the equality of men and women and a spirit of egalitarianism that embraces tolerance, fair play and compassion for those in need". *Waltzing Matilda* meets some of these criteria, but on others it spectacularly fails. Why does he want these values shared? Because "a sense of shared values is our social cement. Without it we risk becoming a society governed by coercion rather than consent." I think he is right about that, too. But perhaps what Mr Howard needs is not history, which resists simplification, but legends: "traditional stories popularly regarded as historical", like the stories and values which cluster so thickly around Anzac Day.

In the last *Quarterly Essay* Amanda Lohrey had this to say about Anzac Day:

> The only collective ripening of emotion, much of it officially nurtured, has been, for better and for worse, the Anzac Story, itself a version of the pre-Christian myth of the young male whose blood in ritual sacrifice is required each spring to fertilise the soil ... In the figure of the Anzac, the sacrifice/crucifixion of the young male god – courtesy of C.E.W. Bean – is secularised and personalised into someone's brother, father, son, grandfather or uncle.

For Lohrey, the power of the Anzac "myth" demonstrates that "the Christian myth is only one of many strains of influence in contemporary Australia culture."

The historian Mark McKenna sees Anzac Day and its multiplying ceremonies differently. In the course of a dynamic lecture delivered in December last year, McKenna pointed to the increasing commercialisation and the political exploitation of "the one day of the year":

> On Anzac Day this year, I walked into my local newsagent to find a card table, draped in a plain white tablecloth, standing in the centre of the shop floor. It was adorned with a selection of Anzac histories – Les Carlyon's *Gallipoli*, Peter FitzSimons's *Kokoda*, Bill Gammage's *The Broken Years* – and other books on Australia's military past. The faces of the diggers – stoic, gaunt and never fearful – stared out from the front covers. In the middle of the table, positioned like a crucifix on an altar, a sign cut from green and gold cardboard read: "Our

Anzacs: Lest We Forget." The shrine was complete. After buying one or two books, customers could then proceed to the counter where they might pick up a small plastic Australian flag, their patriotic purchase accomplished.

A few weeks later McKenna found a poster distributed by the federal government on prominent display in his daughter's primary school (presumably part of that 2004 "values" program) with "words such as 'respect', 'honesty' and 'tolerance' … etched onto a silhouette of Simpson and his donkey. The poor beast now carries not only the wounded and the dying on his back, but a nation's values too." He concludes:

> I walked away from both these encounters realising that I had seen
> local examples of a national phenomenon … The Anzac story has
> now been emptied of its historical context and turned into a sacred
> parable, a hymn of national praise. April 25 has become a day of
> national communion, a day when we bow our heads in remem-
> brance but dare not question the myth.

For McKenna, the cult of Anzac Day demonstrates "the decline of critical history in the public domain". He warns that "more history than ever is today being revised or invented by people who don't want the real past or only a past that suits their purposes. Today is the great age of historical mythology."

My view is different. I think Anzac Day maintains its hold over "the Australian imagination" because it has the plasticity – the openness to personal readings and elaborations – to be constantly renewed. Do I agree with Lohrey's "Spring God" interpretation? There is none of that in my Anzac Day – which does not mean it might not be a dominant theme for others more mystically inclined. As for McKenna's "corruption of history" thesis: I agree that Anzac Day has become the most sacred day in the calendar of this very secular nation. I agree there's a lot of deliberate myth-making about, most of it in high places. But I also think the elasticity of the myth, or, as I would prefer to call it, the legend, of Gallipoli (these are the doings of actual men we are talking about) will confound the manipulators. "The Gallipoli story" lies much closer to historical actuality than do most national myths and legends – as indicated by those history books waiting to be bought in McKenna's local newsagency.

I have read only one of them, Bill Gammage's *The Broken Years*. It is based on the letters and diaries of the men of the 1st AIF, which is about as direct a human-to-human contact as you can get. I hope that people visiting the newsagency that day bought it and read it. It would take them closer to what happened "back then". As for the newsagent: he had taken time and care to assemble his little shrine. Was he only interested in boosting sales? It's a surprisingly wide selection of books. Doesn't that imply a local readership for history books? As for the Simpson poster in the school office: it is true the poster has a mildly sinister history behind it, being part of the federal government's venture into values-promotion in state schools. But is there a better legend for primary-school kids than the story of an unremarkable man called Simpson and his unremarkable donkey who insisted on practising civilian virtues in the middle of a battlefield? In secondary school I would want the poster used as Exhibit A in an enquiry into how and why the legend of "Simpson" was created and disseminated, and why it is being given official backing now. But in primary school? I have to say I am glad to find Simpson and his donkey there.

Anzac Day was created during the great sobering which followed the First World War. That war had been fought in a distant place and for obscure purposes, and its costs were high: 60,000 Australians dead and their graves far away. It was a decisive end to innocence, and the response was accordingly profound. In his classic *Sacred Places*, Ken Inglis tenderly anatomises how Australians mourned and memorialised their dead, individually, locally and collectively, through monuments and through various hand-crafted observances on Anzac and Armistice Day. For the generations who came later, those monuments and observances have taken on new and different meanings.

Mark McKenna is a full generation younger than me, so it was probably the war in Vietnam which has become "War" in his consciousness. I am bound to Anzac Day. I think many thousands of Australians could write an essay on the topic "What Anzac Day Means to Me", and they would all be different. This is mine.

In the late '30s, when I was still too young to count as female (women were of course banned from this sacred men's business), my father used to smuggle me into the Dawn Service at Johnstone's Park in Geelong. My father had not been at Gallipoli, but he had been on the Western Front. I had only the vaguest notion of the history – I knew that there had been a battle, and that we had lost – but I felt and still feel the emotions of the men standing silently around me. One of my few relics is a buff-coloured card from my father's furniture manufactory. It has "From Bench to You" printed on one side, with the factory's address and telephone number, and on the other, in my father's elegant upright hand, this. He must have been going to read it at the Dawn Service:

> Now let us praise famous men, and our fathers that begat us. There be of them that have left a name behind them, that their praises might be reported. And some there be which have no memorial, who are perished as tho' they had never been born, but their glory shall not be blotted out. Their bodies are buried in peace and their name liveth for evermore.

My throat still tightens as I read those words. The sound of a lone bugle, the murmur of magpies in a grey dawn, sweep me back into that strange blend of emotions – pride, grief, anger – as if it were yesterday.

I also remember those two minutes of silence at the eleventh hour of the eleventh day of the eleventh month. I was in Myers on an ordinary morning when the low wail came over the loudspeakers. Chatter stopped. Commerce stopped. The people stood silent, heads bowed, for two long minutes. In the streets the trams stopped, too. That felt like a nation, mourning.

I don't know when Armistice Day was allowed to lapse, but I regret its passing. Now all we have are those old men shyly selling their red-paper poppies in suburban shopping malls, and trying to explain what they mean.

I think it was a good legacy Australians took away from the First World War: a peculiar grace in Australia's way of remembering war as a time for grief and commemoration of loss. Australia celebrates Gallipoli not for its military significance (it was a botched strategy) and not for its cost in numbers dead. Compared to the Somme, it was a sideshow. I haven't read enough of the histories to understand the processes by which this real event was made to resist the erosion of time and to live in our memory, but I suspect it was because the sculpted drama of the setting invited mythification: the beach landing, by untested men; the enemy commanding the heights; the endurance; the seemly withdrawal; the dead abandoned. But I think it was the actual conduct of those men which cemented the Anzac legend. We value these men because they remained steadfast through horror into defeat. Perhaps not all did. But some did. In 1981 the ABC, that indispensable guardian of the nation's history, recorded interviews with a few ageing Anzacs. They seemed to me admirable men – and "admirable" in a distinctive, instantly recognisable, Australian style. Am I being manipulated? Possibly. But I doubt it.

As for the nation's political health: contrast Anzac Day with the stories Germans made to console themselves after the defeat of 1918. I think our mode of celebrating Anzac Day is unparalleled in its sober mourning for young lives lost, wasted, broken. There is no triumphalism about it. For me, then and now, the giant question "Gallipoli" and its commemorations raise is "Why?" Why this waste, with the reasons for battle so tenuous, and the deaths so real? It is only now that I realise that it was my childhood awareness of the horror and the pity of war which determined the focus of my later work, as I struggle to understand the social and psychological forces which can lead men into the organised violence of war, and then keep them there.

Anzac Day is for me, as I think it is for many Australians, a personal possession. It holds my childhood memories of family and neighbourhood, when war was at once distant and immanent. That is how ritual works, as a portmanteau of past experience and of present emotion. Like most of my generation, I am practised in irony, but I feel no irony about Anzac Day.

Naturally, therefore, I am offended by change. I am almost as conservative as the RSL about that, for much the same reasons. But time tirelessly attacks the rituals we design to arrest it. As Humphrey McQueen neatly put it (on 25 April 2003), "Anzac Day has never been what it used to be."

Anzac Day is still changing. This year the usual controversy over who should be allowed to march focused on the possibility of "Johnny Turk" marching alongside Australian soldiers. The RSL backed the inclusion. The Turks, we were told, were honourable enemies. Remembering the Armenians, we flinch. But we are bound to the Turks not only because they cared for our dead, but also because they were there. They had seen the Anzacs in hallowed action. If Turks, who were enemies, why not Italians, now a large and loved component of Australian society? Why not any soldier from any war? But an inclusive march could risk changing "our" Anzac Day into a mere military parade, a general celebration of war – or even a mute demonstration against war. The RSL does not want "war" considered in the abstract. It is our wars they want commemorated. Above all they want our youth, resident or incoming, to share the older generation's feelings about this most special moment in this most special war.

Of course it can't be done, any more than women could be kept out of the march and applauding meekly from the sidelines. I don't much like the changes – the flag-waving, the general cheerfulness which has displaced the mournful dignity of "my" Anzac Day. I especially disliked the incorporation of Anzac Cove as a must-see destination on Australian backpackers' standard world tour. I thought the combination of cheap air travel and the kitsch which swamps sacred places that are also places of commercial opportunity would do for our sacred legend. Then I read what some of those backpackers had to say about their "Gallipoli experience" (an historian had taken the trouble to ask them, and to record what they said) and realised, yet again, as they groped for words to describe the unfamiliar emotions which had engulfed them, that every generation will take the old legends and make them real: that Anzac Day is no longer mine, but theirs.

Would more concentration on Anzac Day in the schools help that natural evolution? I doubt it. The interest groups resisting the recognition of change are simply too powerful to allow it. In the *Age* of 17 April this year, it was reported that the RSL in the person of a member of its Victorian executive wants more emphasis in schools on teaching war history, and that he and his RSL comrades stand ready to help, because "Schools have definitely got to get it right." Which means, of course, RSL right. There is not likely to be much emphasis on the different grounds and different degrees of legitimacy of different wars. To the RSL all wars our boys fought in are just, because they fought in them.

Can the layered histories contained in Anzac Day commemorations be inserted into the awareness of recent migrants to this country? They have their own wars to remember. But the loss of young men dead in battle is a universal grief, and their mourning a universal practice. I think Anzac Day will expand to include them. It will certainly die without them.

I hope enough of the tone of our old Anzac legend will survive to rebuke the temptation to glamorise war we see indulged so exuberantly in the United States of America (compare the very different demeanours of the American President and our Prime Minister in the presence of "fighting men"). Despite its increasing militarisation and commercialisation, Anzac Day is still a mourning ceremony, regularly reminding us that war is a bad business. Peter Cosgrove, a military man with the most unmilitary virtue of publicly worrying over the welfare of the men and women under his command, enjoys near-universal popularity and trust.

He is about as far from the macho military man as you can get. I think the Anzac tradition has more than a little to do with that.

Ceremonies arouse strong emotions. They will always be areas of contest (consider the lurid history of the "proper" shape of the Catholic Mass). The plasticity of Anzac Day observances worries some historians, in part because they (reasonably) mistrust the political thrust behind some of the changes, but also because they underestimate the natural dynamism of popular ritual observance. Story-spinning dismays people committed to notions of accuracy and evidence.

Other Australian historians have done fine work on Anzac Day, lovingly retrieving the history of what happened, then tracing how that history was worked upon by a range of interest groups to be made into something else. Given that legends and rituals are attempts not only to memorialise a moment from the past, but also to stimulate and direct emotions now, that is a valuable exercise.

It is one we might recall in view of the challenge to historians' role as custodians and interpreters of the past now being mounted by Australian novelists. It is to that dispute I now turn.

Novelists writing on historical topics and historians writing history used to jog along their adjacent paths reasonably companionably. More recently, perhaps because the intra-disciplinary disarray of the history wars has awakened imperial ambitions, novelists have been doing their best to bump historians off the track. It seems that that they have decided it is for them to write the history of this country, and to admonish and nurture its soul.

In his essay "How Sorry Can We Be?" in *Sense & Nonsense in Australian History*, John Hirst forcefully rejects fiction writers' claim to write more penetrating history than historians. Hirst had been particularly provoked by the expansive claims Kate Grenville has been making for her novel *The Secret River*, and states his objections with his usual vigour.

I have to confess that I found *The Secret River* difficult to read, unlike all Grenville's other novels. This was in part because, having recently written out of the same sources, I flinched from what looked like opportunistic transpositions and elisions. I was also taken aback by the novel's portentous tone: this was not the Grenville I was used to. Worst, from the opening gambit (worthy fellow, trivial offence, transportation to Botany Bay) I was pretty sure I knew the plot; when the worthy fellow took up land on the Hawkesbury and saw those shadows flitting behind the trees, I was sure of it. Historians are puritans when it comes to the novelisation of history, and in what follows I will try to explain why, taking Grenville as my example not because she is the worst offender, but because she has thought hard about what she is doing and is ready to talk about it frankly.

To begin with a flashback: after she had published *The Idea of Perfection* and when she was just embarking on research into her ancestor Solomon Wiseman (splendidly improbable name), Grenville took part in a seminar with historians at the National Library in Canberra. She titled her talk, with typical élan, "The Novelist as Barbarian". Why "barbarian"? Because *as a novelist, my relationship to history has always been pretty much the same relationship* the Goths had to Rome. History for a greedy novelist like me is just one more place to pillage ... What we're after, of course, is stories ... Having found them, we then proceed to fiddle with them to make them the way we want them to be, rather than the way they really were. We get it wrong, wilfully and knowingly ... My epiphany ... was reading Manning Clark. Here was an historian not hiding behind a mask of "objectivity" but being shamelessly personal ... If I thought, in my ignorance, that I was going to put the "story" back into "history", I had to recognise that he had already done it, with a breadth of vision and depth of knowledge no novelist could match.

Back then Grenville thought of the past as a story-bank. She also thought novelists could not write history, and that the historian could trump the novelist as story finder and teller provided he was "shamelessly personal" and had given up any pretence of "objectivity", which for Grenville is an illusion. (Note too, for future reference, the assumption that history is, or ought to be, about finding and telling stories.)

Like everybody embarking on a new project, Grenville fantasised a general reformation of work methods: I'll be orderly and systematic. I'll find out everything there is to know about Solomon Wiseman. But she knew her novelist's nature: In fact, of course, I suspect I'll do my usual smash-and-grab raid on history. I'll research only until I find something juicy, and then I'll run off with it and turn it into something else.

Then during her research for the The Secret River Grenville experienced a deeper epiphany. She discovered she could write history after all. The novel is a serious attempt to do history, but value-added history: history given life and flesh by a novelist's imagination. Grenville sees her novel as a work of history sailing triumphantly beyond the constrictions of the formal discipline of history-writing.

In early 2006, Grenville was interviewed by Ramona Koval on Radio National. Koval's first question was about literary technique: how to represent direct speech. Grenville's answer: italicise: in Lillian's Story, my first novel, I used italics for dialogue, and I felt happy with it. (I thought the technique worked beautifully in that novel, so I have borrowed it to represent Grenville's speech here.)

First reflection: historians don't have this problem because historians can't do conversations at all. They can manage the occasional ejaculation – "Liberty or Death!" "Aux Armes!" They can even more occasionally do last words: "Such is life." They can sometimes make monologues out of formal speeches or secret diaries or confessional statements. But the informal verbal interactions of daily life? No. They are lost to us.

There was also the problem of "voice" for those imagined conversations: *I needed a voice that was kind of plausible for* [the main character] *Thornhill … What I ended up with was something that was fairly plain. The vocabulary is quite plain, the syntax is quite plain, but I hope that by arranging quite plain words in perhaps slightly unusual ways, I would get a slightly antique feeling and also a plausible voice for this Thames bargeman … Every now and again I drop in a slightly antique word like "britches" or "vittles" and hope, also, that that gives a kind of antique flavour without being literally "ye olde".* Reflection: this simulation of appropriate speech styles is an enduring problem for novelists. It is not a problem for historians because either they are using their own ordinary language, or quoting directly from contemporary documents.

Grenville's theme: *What I wanted to describe or suggest was the fact that Australian history does have a series of secrets in it.* On this claim I refer readers to the critiques of John Hirst and Mark McKenna, both distinguished historians of Australia as I am not. Grenville's thesis: *In doing all the research for this book, what I came away with overwhelmingly was the feeling that there had been no particular ill-will on both sides, at least in the beginning, but a complete inability to communicate. So it was a tragic, tragic inability to communicate across a gulf of culture.* I arrived at much the same conclusion in *Dancing with Strangers*, although I would want to change that "complete" to "defective". And is the outcome adequately described as "tragic"? Tragic it certainly was. But it could so easily have been worse.

Then divergences begin to widen. Koval: "Did settlers regard Aborigines as non-human?" Grenville: *a few might have thought that, but most did not.* But how can we know whether "most " or "few"? Some confident psychological analysis follows: *[Settlers] allowed themselves to get into a kind of* rationalisation about the Aborigines' attitude to land. They allowed themselves to pretend that because the Aborigines were nomads, they therefore had no particular attachment to place. But it was a real schizophrenia because at the very same moment ... when you read the research you see this double-think going on ... they could ... recognise that Aborigines burst into cries of joy when they were returned to their own place ... so I think there was a huge double-think going on.

Grenville concludes, therefore, that the tragedy could have been avoided: You want to go back 200 years and say to the settlers, "Look, this is how the Aborigines are," and to the Aborigines, "Look, this is why the settlers are behaving the way they are. Let's understand this. There's no need for all this brutality." The novelist has decided that violence was unnecessary: that the contest over the land, being due to a failure of communication, could have been resolved by discussion. The historian asks: given the incompatible uses to which the land was to be put, how could violence have been avoided?

Grenville reveals a contemporary delicacy of mind when she declares she will not attempt to enter the minds of her Aboriginal characters, first because of political sensibility (there has been enough appropriation already) but also because that's not a story I could tell. I do believe that you have to draw on what you know to write well, and I don't pretend to understand or be able to empathise particularly with a tribal Aboriginal person from 200 years ago; that's beyond me. Yet she acknowledges no such difficulty empathising with assorted Britishers from 200 years ago, stepping so confidently into their minds that she is ready to diagnose not only "double-think", which might be inferred from incompatible statements and incoherent responses, but "paranoia".

Then came the passage which must have annoyed every historian who read it. Asked where she stood on the history wars, Grenville said she was up on a stepladder, looking down on the historians battling away below about the details of exactly when and where and how many and how much, and they've got themselves into these polarised positions ... but a novelist can stand up on a stepladder and look down at this, outside the fray, and say there is another way to understand it. You can set two sides against each other and ask which side will win ... or you can go up on the stepladder and look down and say, well, nobody is going to win. And then: Once *you can actually get inside the experience, it's no longer a matter of who's going to win, it's simply a matter of yes, now I understand both sides.*

Novelists "can actually get inside the experience"; historians do not and cannot; historians are in a constant state of affray. Grenville concludes with a statement about her method: *The historians are doing their thing, but let me as a novelist come to it in a different way, which is the way of empathising and imaginative understanding of those difficult events.* How will she do that? *Basically to think, well, what would I have done in that situation, and what sort of a person would that make me?*

So here we have it: Grenville's secret method for penetrating British minds – although not Aboriginal ones, which must remain forever closed to us – is Applied Empathy: the peculiar talent of the novelist to penetrate other minds through exercising her imagination upon fragmentary, ambiguous, sometimes contradictory evidence. Grenville's claim to "know" with *equal certainty* both what is intimated within the records, and what is beyond it, exposes the gulf between "doing history" and "doing fiction". Consider the difference between a great novel like John Banville's *The Untouchable*, arising from contemplation of the strange life of the art connoisseur/spy Anthony Blunt, and a great biography, Barry Hill's *Broken Song: T.G.H. Strehlow and Aboriginal Possession*, provoked by contemplation of the strange life of Ted Strehlow, anthropologist. Banville offers an interior monologue, undulating somewhere in the vicinity of the ascertainable facts, but going far beyond them. Hill offers a sustained, tender investigation into the known facts of Strehlow's life. When he moves beyond them into untestable speculation, he tells us so. Historians are the permanent spoilsports of imaginative games played with the past. Why? For the following reasons.

What would I have done in that situation, and what sort of a person would that make me? Grenville would not have been Grenville in "that situation". We cannot post ourselves back in time. People really did think differently then – or at least we must proceed on that assumption. Nor can we restrict our efforts towards understanding only to those people we guess to be approximately of our own kind, because that would condemn us to playing Blind Man's Bluff in a largely unintelligible world.

Grenville's is not a new position. Mark McKenna quotes David Malouf from a decade ago:

> Our only way of grasping our history – and by history I really mean what has happened to us, and what determines what we are now and where we are now – the only way of really coming to terms with that is by people's entering into it in their imagination, not by the world of facts, but by being there. And the only thing really which puts you there in that kind of way is fiction ... It's when you have actually been there and become a character again in that world ...

For Malouf, as for Grenville, historians create only a "world of facts"; novelists so stimulate our imaginations that we think we are actually there. And for him, too, the empathetic experience is redemptive: "I keep wanting to say societies can only become whole, can only know fully what they are, when they have relived history in that kind of way."

Some engaged reading, some preliminary flexing of the imagination, a run, a vault, and presto! you are there. How do you know you are now in the Past? Because while the place might look exotic, you understand it so much better than the complicated place in which you usually live. In the novelist's "past" everyone behaves delightfully "in character", and everyone submits to the plot. The novelist might surprise her readers. She will never surprise herself.

By contrast, the real past is surrounded by prickle-bushes of what I have to call epistemological difficulties. (From a handy online dictionary: "In a nutshell, epistemology addresses the questions, 'Do you really know what you think you know?'" You do epistemology all the time – as when you assess the likely truth of a rich piece of gossip.) Access to the actual past is slow, always problematic, and its inhabitants can be relied on to affront our expectations. I was cured of any residual faith in the utility of empathy by spending rather more than a decade in company with Aztecs. I knew they were human. I was reminded of that a dozen times a day. But it quickly became obvious that their minds and their emotions were ordered differently from mine. This meant that if I were to penetrate any distance at all into the Aztec world of the imagination, I would have to keep my own imagination on a very short leash, because my imagination, like my emotions and assumptions, has grown organically out of my own experiences within my own cultural milieu.

One example only: I could "follow" the typical Aztec childbirth scene easily enough – the mother-to-be cosseted through pregnancy, then helped through the birth by skilled women, then feted as the entire extended kin came trooping into the domestic courtyard to praise her and to greet the new baby. The newborn, naked, was handed around to each member of the family to be stroked and cuddled while the formula of welcome was recited. (I was especially touched by the image of the scarred arms of warriors cradling the tiny baby.) Then if the baby were male, the chief midwife would take it, elevate it to the gods and dedicate it to a warrior's death on the killing-stone. With that action a mist dropped: a mist which would only be dispersed, and then only partially, by long, cautious labour. Untutored "subjectivity", "empathy", was of not the least use to me inside the Aztec world. Indulged, it would have destroyed all hope of understanding.

How close can we draw to alien minds? Consider the torture scene in Brian Moore's Black Robe, his novel about the experiences of a Jesuit sent as a missionary to the Huron Indians of seventeenth-century Canada. Moore took every hideous detail of the scene from a rock-solid historical source: the eyewitness account of a (stunningly cool) Jesuit. We know that these events really happened. Can empathy help us "become a character" in the Huron world? We might scuttle along behind the action striking Huron attitudes, but neither we nor Moore will understand what these fellow humans thought they were up to. We have to be content to watch: to think, "How terrible. How strange."

Anthropologists can sometimes draw closer. What did Ilongot men of only a generation ago feel when, having taken the head of an enemy (man, woman or child), they would toss the head in the air, catch it, and toss it again? It was clearly an emotionally charged experience. But how to discover how those emotions could be described, how they were stimulated, what they signified, why they were cherished? It took American anthropologist Michelle Rosaldo months of watching, questioning and watching again to arrive at sufficient understanding of Ilongot culture to be able to write her classic *Knowledge and Passion*, where she tentatively reconstructs the sequence of emotions experienced by triumphant head-takers, and the complex reading of the world which informed it. Physically she was "there". She could live among her people. (As it happened, she would also die among them, falling to her death from a narrow walking-track.) But she knew she could not intuit what was in their minds. For that she needed long observation, cool thought and the constant awareness that her own intuitions could be of no use at all.

If empathy cannot be made to serve outsiders living among particular people now, how can it be expected to serve historians or novelists distanced by time, space and culture from the people they are seeking to understand? Grenville might reasonably complain that she acknowledged empathy to be culture-bound by her refusal to try to penetrate the otherness of Aborigines. But she felt no such inhibition about claiming to penetrate the minds of British convict-keepers, convicts and settlers of 200 years ago, even to the extent of diagnosing the pathological mental condition she thought she found there. So the question is: how much "culture" do we really share with British people of 200 years ago? Are we seduced into an illusion of understanding through the accident of a shared language?

To test that possibility I need to analyse one small episode. (It is possible I am being unreasonably stern about this, but I have no intention of being left down at the foot of the ladder squabbling with Windschuttle.) At the beginning of the Koval interview Grenville read a passage in which her normally tough protagonist is badly frightened when he is taken by a sea-seasoned friend out of Sydney Harbour and into Broken Bay with big seas running. The passage is beautifully described; Grenville has a right to be proud of it. Koval asked how she came to do it. *I read everything I could read about everything that was relevant to the book, even obliquely relevant, including boats and ships [but] of course, you can only get a certain amount out of books. Basically you've got to go out there and experience it.* She tells us how she herself had experienced a turn into Broken Bay on a day of heavy swell ...

I took the ferry across from Palm Beach to Ettalong one day, and it happened to be really rough, and it's just a public ferry, it's no big deal. But I was terrified. I was gripping the gunwale like Thornhill, and I suddenly tasted the salt on my lips, and I realised that I was more frightened than I had been for many years. One part of me was frightened, and the other part was cold-bloodedly taking notes in my notebook. This is what fear feels like. So as much as I could in the book, I did everything that I had to describe. Grenville sums up: *I'm a great believer in the experiential theory of writing.*

I'm a great believer in the experiential theory of writing. Grenville therefore bestows her experiences from that rough ferry trip from Ettalong – terror, salt on the lips – on the boatman Thornhill. Is this a legitimate transference? As it happens, we have a close account of a passage out between North and South Head with a big sea running from a marine lieutenant named Ralph Clark. This time there is no problem of artificially archaising the language. The spellings, misspellings and the punctuation are Clark's:

> Saterday 6th (March 1790) About Six o'Clock got under way a great Swell Setting into the Harbour – just as we came abreast of the outer South Head it fell calm and the Swell was setting us fast to leward on the North Head which had not a puff of wind fild the Sails we should have been drove on Shore on the North Head and every body on board thought of no other but that we should – if we had the Ship would have been in pices in a few minutes from the great

Sea that was breaking on the Rocks and most of use on board would
have been lost but by great good fortune the puff of wind Shoved
use clear out of the harbour … I have been very Sick all day.

Grenville had been in a stabilised vessel; Clark had taken a prolonged
tossing: there was vomit as well as salt on his lips. Grenville was in a pow-
ered vessel in radio contact with the shore; Thornhill and Clark were at
the mercy of wave and wind, with no help in prospect. We can identify
those material differences. Mental differences are more difficult to measure. Grenville felt fear, and tells us so. Can we say confidently that Clark
felt "fear"? He might have been afraid. We would expect him to be afraid.
But what his words suggest is that he was engrossed in analysing the situation and calculating the chances. Men like Clark, a "sea-soldier" – men
like the fictional character "Thornhill", who had survived the long, peril-
ous voyage to Australia – were more familiar with rough seas and with
danger than we are. Can we really read off their moods and reactions
from our own?

The ship which took Clark out through the Heads on that providential
"puff of wind", the *Sirius*, the pride of the tiny British fleet, would not
make landfall. It was tossed onto the reef at Norfolk Island by another
freak wind, and there held fast. As the ship began to break up, Clark, who
had got ashore earlier, went out on a makeshift raft to help save whatever
people and provisions he could. A convict pressed into service panicked,
tumbled Clark off the raft and then fell in after him. The man couldn't
swim: Clark had to swim to the beach through heavy surf, with the convict clinging to his belt.

This is what happened next: "When I got on Shore he was almost dead
but he Soon Recovered on which I took a Stick out of one of the Serjeants
hands and gave him a damned good thrashing for pulling me of the Raft
with him – he better have been drown for I will give his the Same every
day for this month to come that I meet him." The same language? Yes. But
we are in another country.

Clark would be dead within three years of that taxing swim, killed fighting the French in Haiti. His young son Ralphie, nine years old and newly enlisted in the Marines, was probably already dead of fever. Clark died too soon to receive the news that his beloved wife had died in child-birth back in England, and that the baby was dead too. Two hundred years ago people were more familiar with death than we are. Death, pain and violence were always at their elbow. With Aztecs, those three pres-ences cast their long shadows over the joy of a successful birth. That alone makes me unwilling to impose our conveniently simplified alpha-bet of emotions – "fear", "pity", "anger" – on them. These are turbid waters, not to be explored here. But the cocoon of physical security in which we live might be our greatest barrier to understanding how it was for other people of other times, or how it is for people in other places now. That massive change in circumstance alone renders the hope of "empathy" a fiction.

Notice, too, that while it is possible to disagree with me as to what happened during that Norfolk Island shipwreck and what to make of it, it is not possible to disagree with Grenville, because it is her own self-created world that we are visiting.

As for the self-denying ordinance against employing the empathetic technique on Aboriginal Australians: it is no simple thing to fathom some-thing of what the Australians around what became "Sydney" thought about the white incomers, especially when we are effectively limited to the journals written by those same incomers, but I hope I demonstrated in *Dancing with Strangers* that with patience, attentiveness and sufficient test-ing of the ground it is possible to penetrate a little distance. And surely "alien cultures" are everywhere? Will my narrow experience help me penetrate the thinking of, say, a widow with five children living on the seventh floor of a Housing Commission flat? A man who enjoys peder-asty? That girl with the embroidered belly-button and the long cuts on her forearms?

Above all: how am I to test my guesses? However seductive they might be, the "insights" of empathy are untestable. The philosopher of history Louis Mink puts the point neatly:

> It is misleading to say that in order to understand Caesar's decision to cross the Rubicon I must somehow "become" Caesar or "relive" his decision. Obviously I can imagine myself as Caesar no matter how little I know about him, and such imagination is worthless from the standpoint of knowledge, though it has produced some interesting imaginative dramas.

Most important: an unexamined confidence in empathy tempts us to deny the possibility of significant difference. This encourages the identification of those who persist in being different from us – people who fail "the empathy test" – as evil, or even as less than human. We all know the consequences of that.

It is true that historians are cruelly limited. We can't do conversations; we can't (usually) do monologues. But what we can do is become increasingly knowledgeable about the contexts in which particular actions, including the writing of particular words, took place. We do this not by empathetic time-leaps, which would condemn us to live forever sealed into our own narrow cultural and temporal world, but by reconstructing as delicately, as comprehensively and as subtly as we are able, not only the material but also the cultural settings in which other people, once living, now dead, lived out their lives.

For an analogy for this process, consider the way novices like me watched the World Cup soccer. Watching over time, and with a little help from my friends, I could fathom the rules of the game, and even identify some of the conventional ways of breaking them. I was beginning to recognise the beginnings of offensive plays and the shapes of defensive responses. I even glimpsed the deep mythic/historic background ("Like Maradonna!"). I was still a long way from playing the game.

Historical novelists spend time getting the material setting right, but then, misled by their confidence in their novelist's gift of empathetic imagination, they sometimes project back into that carefully constructed material setting contemporary assumptions and current obsessions. I think that is what happened to that fine novelist Kate Grenville when she wrote *The Secret River.*

In 1901 the aspiring novelist Sarah Orne Jewett bravely sent Henry James a copy of her new novel, *The Tory Lover.* On 5 October James replied, and poor Miss Jewett got more than anyone could have bargained for. After some preliminary cozening ("charming touch, tact and taste … a woman of genius and courage") James transforms into the great, ruthless critic he is:

> The 'historical novel' is, for me, condemned, even in cases of labour as delicate as yours, to a fatal *cheapness*, for the simple reason that the difficulty of the job is inordinate and that a mere *escamotage*, in the interest of ease, and of the abysmal public *naiveté*, becomes inevitable. You may multiply the little facts that can be got from pictures and documents, relics and prints, as much as you like – the real thing is almost impossible to do, and in its essence the whole effect is as nought: I mean the invention, the representation of the old CONSCIOUSNESS, the soul, the sense, the horizon, the vision of individuals in whose minds half the things that make ours, that make the modern world were non-existent. You have to think with your modern apparatus a man, a woman – or rather fifty – whose own thinking was intensely otherwise conditioned, you have to simplify back by an amazing *tour de force* – and even then it's all humbug … You, I hasten to add, seem to me to have steered very clear of [these ineptitudes] – to have seen your work very bravely and to have handled it firmly; but even you court disaster by composing the whole thing so much by sequences of speeches.

Kate Grenville has "seen her work bravely" and "handled it firmly". But James's century-old strictures still apply.

Nonetheless, and in the face of all the above, I have to grant that some novelists write gripping novels which also inform us about the past. My favourite, J.G. Farrell's *The Siege of Krishnapur*, is fastidiously researched and even more fastidiously imagined. He creates his main character, the superbly-whiskered Collector of Taxes for the Raj at Krishnapur, out of the dense biographical data we have on other Englishmen in that position and in that period. But he does not do anything so dull as make him "typical": his Collector is realistically idiosyncratic, and unexpectedly loveable. As for the setting: the physical milieu is established, brilliantly, over the first couple of pages; the social milieu slowly, delicately over time. There is no time-travel here, and not the least glint of modern sensibilities. Through long research and longer reflection Farrell has equipped his characters with sensibilities appropriate to their particular time, station and experience of life.

Then – having done all this good history – Farrell kicks loose, inventing things which might have happened but we don't know did, because they are the kinds of things that records always miss. He shows us how the British characters and their relationships changed as the siege tightened; how some genteel protocols were abandoned and others passionately sustained; how a plump would-be poet transformed into a lithe green-clad hero and then reverted. He does some entrancing conversations; he injects the climactic battle scene with mad hilarity. He chooses to leave the Indian "mutineers" out except for a couple the British view as comical. The rest are left a menacing roar offstage, until they erupt from the wings. I doubt Farrell left the Indians out because he thought he could not "empathise" with them. He could have researched the general and made the particulars up, as he did with his equally exotic British characters. I think he decided they would unduly clutter the stage. He is concerned with drama and with comedy, not with rebuking the insults and the extravagances of imperialism – although as we watch his British in bumbling action we wonder how the Raj could have lasted so long.

The novel is exhilarating to read, and at the end of it we have an expanded sense of how it might have been over those last weeks for the dwindling British contingent at Krishnapur. But that is a bonus. What we have been enjoying is an elegant display of art, tempered by historical considerations, but restricted neither by them nor by the limits of the extant documentation. Farrell chooses to make his Collector sympathetic, chooses to leave the Indians out, chooses to present scenes of slaughter as high farce, because he is busy confecting a comedy of British manners out of the terrible realities of the Siege of Krishnapur.

What Australian history book could I put up against a gripping historical novel for excitement and illumination? Out of several contenders I nominate Don Watson's *Caledonia Australis: Scottish Highlanders on the Frontier of Australia*, which pursues the same theme as Grenville's *The Secret River*: the clearing of blacks from contested land. Watson is always being identified as "Paul Keating's biographer" or "Max Gillies' scriptwriter" or "the author of *Weasel Words*", but not as the author of what might be the best ethnographic history of an Australian frontier encounter, when Scots Highlanders evicted from their traditional lands arrived in what would become Gippsland, and proceeded to evict the traditional owners from theirs, employing all necessary ferocity, and then to establish a seemly, godly society with the handful of Kurnai survivors transformed into indulged dependants, Highland style. It is a close-to-incredible story. Were it invented, we would dismiss it as implausible, but Watson tells it through so patient and considered an accretion of detail that we have no choice: as we close the book we say: "So that's how it was." We also say: "How extraordinary. Who could have believed it?" But we do believe it, because the evidence is telling and the arguments good.

So Grenville is right. Historians do have the best stories. Who would dare invent The Black Hole of Calcutta? Who would invent The Cane Toad story, or what happened when the juvenile offender Peter Rabbit was transported to the Antipodes?

History also enjoys the advantage, and the burden, of dealing with the real. Farrell could make comic art out of terrible events, just as Nabokov made art, drama, comedy and pathos out of a ruthless man's exploitation of his child slave. That is the novelist's prerogative. Nabokov and Farrell widen our sense of what humans might be capable. Historians are concerned with what men and women have actually done. It is historians who are left to explain how it could be that a decade ago two little Belgian girls, eight years old, could have been kidnapped, raped and kept in a cellar, and then left to starve when their jailer was jailed for a minor offence.

Novelists enjoy their space for invention because their only binding contract is with their readers, and that ultimately is not to instruct or to reform, but to delight. They create whole worlds for us to play in. They also flirt with actuality. They might choose to make their puppets dance on the very edge of the history–fiction ravine: to present living people "disguised" under a different name. That is risky. The victim might choose to sue. By contrast, the dead can be traduced, parodied or exalted at will. They have no protection beyond what might be provided by their historian defenders. But should an historian protest, "But she/he was not like that at all, and I can prove it," the novelists, indeed the whole legion of litterateurs, will roar in chorus: "Irrelevant! This is a novel, stupid!" That practised slither between "this is a serious work of history" and "judge me only on my literary art" has always annoyed me.

Some novelists, may their tribe increase, refuse to slither. They step delicately, firmly within their chosen domain. Margaret Atwood, surefooted in this as in other matters, tells us how she wrote her *Alias Grace* in an "Historical Afterword". There really was once a young woman called "Grace" who was tried for the murder of her employer. Atwood decided to make a novel out of those beginning clues. She researched everything she could research about her character's social context – the immigrant ship, terms of employment for Irish immigrant domestic servants, the degree of sexual vulnerability of a young woman in domestic service in that particular place at that particular time; on what principles and assumptions courts of law and asylums were run according to what models of mental derangement. And then she says: "We don't know anything about what happened to Grace after she was sentenced, so from now on I'm going to make it up." Which she most memorably does.

Closer to home: Tom Keneally makes artlessness an art form in his novel *The Playmaker*, which stars a marine lieutenant called "Ralph Clark". Is he the Ralph Clark we met going out through the heads? Well – no. But then again ... he could be (see the "Author's Note" at the close of the novel). Peter Carey won my heart at a Brisbane Writers' Festival a few years ago when a string of people were interrogating him about *The True History of the Kelly Gang*. As the session went on, the interrogation became increasingly hostile. I have forgotten the questions, but I have not forgotten the tone: "On what grounds did you de-emphasise Kelly's uncle's association with the police? What evidence do you have for the Green Sash affair? How do you justify your claims as to the time taken to get from Jerilderie to Whoopty Doo on an average-to-good horse?" And Carey would slide further and further down into his chair and say: "I made it up." His interrogators were insisting he had written history. He knew he had written fiction. Carey, whose inventive powers are uninhibited, who aims at transformation, not replication of the past or reformation of the present – and who is so confident of his footing on his edge of the ravine to caper on it – put the matter crisply back in 1997: "It doesn't matter what is out in the real world: this is art and you are making it to suit your needs."

More Henry James, this time from his *The Art of Fiction*: "The only obligation to which in advance we may hold a novel ... is that it be interesting." Interesting. It need not, indeed ought not, be "true", because truth inhibits art.

Novelists claim that a) people-making and b) fluent storytelling can't be done by historians, or if they can, fiction does it better.

I think those claims must be granted. Think of *Anna Karenina*. Leo Tolstoy, not yet the greybeard seer tottering through snow but a robust man in his fifties, knows this woman so completely that he can control the pace and process of our access to her. We are as intrigued by her first appearance as is Vronski, as dazzled by her radiant serenity, and we remain dazzled over many pages because we cannot see her clearly. We come to know her slowly, because this is a woman of depths unknown even to herself. In time we see her in her raging, insupportable anguish, and learn, as she is learning, the destruction of which she is capable. By contrast we are on easy terms with her endearingly carnal, irresponsible brother, Oblonski, within two minutes of meeting him. We know what to expect of him. We know he will offend again, we hope Dolly will always forgive him, and we will always be glad to see him.

It is this magisterial control over character and action which marks the great novelist, and no historian could conceivably match it. Nabokov, who is on my side if for different reasons and who is also looking for trouble, elaborates the point by way of a "real" historical figure, one Count Beust, who briefly turns up in *Anna Karenina*:

> To make his magic, fiction, look real the artist sometimes places it, as Tolstoy does, within a definite, specific historical frame, citing facts that can be checked in a library – that citadel of illusion … The case of Count Beust is an excellent example to bring into any discussion about so-called real life and so-called fiction. There is on one hand an historical fact, a certain Beust, a statesman, a diplomat, who not only existed but has left a book of memoirs in two volumes, wherein he carefully recalls all the witty repartees, and political puns, which he made in the course of his long political career on this or that occasion. [Unstated: who would put this insupportably dreary fellow in a novel?] And here, on the other hand, is Steve Oblonski whom Tolstoy created from top to toe, and the question is which of the two, the "real-life" Count Beust, or the "fictitious" Prince Oblonski is more alive, is more real, is more believable.

The ace slams into court; the "real" contender is left flat-footed, humiliated, ridiculous.

Nabokov is being more than a little shifty here, stealing "real" to equate with "magically realistic". It might also be possible to come up with some trivial defence – "Beust may have been just as charming as Oblonski while he was being shaved, it's just that we don't know" – but it's limp, and we know it. "Real" in the sense of "true to life" is an epithet much more easily applied to the novel than to a history, first because novelists are not earth-and-evidence bound, and also because they can impose a shapeliness on chaotic experience which elevates it into parable mode. That shapeliness facilitates not only character-creation, but compelling story-making. Philip Roth: "I read fiction to be freed from my own suffocatingly narrow perspective on life and to be lured into imaginative sympathy with a fully developed narrative point of view not my own. It's the same reason that I write."

That freedom has large consequences. First, we expect the novelist's creations and narratives to delight us. That is their proper task. We expect them to be coherent in a way we do not expect of real life – which we would reject in real life as unrealistically tidy. If they are chaotic, we must believe the chaos is a deliberate effect. More important: because we know these creations are fictions, we readers relate to them differently both aesthetically and morally than we do to what is declared to be non-fiction.

It is that confusion between the primarily aesthetic purpose of fiction and the primarily moral purpose of history which makes the present jostling for territory matter. Some readers might think that my "ravine" – the gulf between writing imaginative fiction and writing evidence-bound history – is no more than a dent in the topsoil, or possibly only a line scratched in sand by historians desperate to defend their territory. But readers clearly do care about the truth-status of what they are reading. Consider again the fuss over "Helen Demidenko". When it was realised that she was not the daughter of a fascist Ukrainian taxi-driver thoroughly steeped in the Ukrainian view of the world, her words on the page –

words she had officially declared to be fictitious — remained unchanged. But her covert claim had been that they had come directly out of her own authentic experience, and they instantly lost their power to compel.

The movement can go the other way: people were even more eager to read the lush fictions of *The Bride Stripped Bare* when they thought it was "really" the author in there under the covers, blushing and pulling the sheet up over her head. I think those responses arise out of the recognition of the different moral contracts established between writer, reader and subject in the two genres. Consider again how we feel about Anna Karenina, this woman we come to know so well. We don't want her to say: "I must be crazy, trading my reliable husband, my charming home, my darling boy, for a big moustache and a military cloak"; to give up Vronski and live on to comfortable grandmotherhood. We want her dead under that train. We will weep for her. But they will be luxurious, indulgent tears, shed as we contemplate the tragic parabola of her life. We would not have it different. If we knew a real Anna, we would be tugging desperately at her sleeve.

Three years ago the novelist Kate Jennings had this to say about the difference between fiction and non-fiction: "My job as a novelist is to explore human behaviour, the personal and the public, to join intellect with emotion — in a way that non-fiction writers can't."

Only novelists can "join intellect with emotion"? I thought a documentarian named Primo Levi managed to do that rather well. Perhaps Jennings might say that autobiographical writing is a special case because there "intellect" and "emotion" become fused. But are they ever separable?

Back to Henry James's *Art of Fiction*: "Experience is never limited, and it is never complete; it is an immense sensibility, a kind of huge spider-web of the finest silken threads suspended in the chamber of consciousness, and catching every air-borne particle in its tissue." Then comes one of his few exhortations: "Try to be one of the people on whom nothing is lost!"

True, James is talking about the creation of fiction. But acute sensibility is not manifested exclusively by fiction-writers writing fiction. Consider the incandescent letters of Gustave Flaubert, or Ivan Turgenev's eyewitness account of the guillotining of a young murderer called Tropman. Nothing is "lost" on them. Closer to home: one of the several qualities which makes Helen Garner's non-fiction writing great is her unflinching vulnerability. She tells us with all the honesty she can muster the rush of sensations and memories induced by donning a fencing mask, playing with a grand-daughter, taking a walk with a penguin on an Antarctic beach. For Garner authentic emotions provide the living tissue for the play of intellect. This is surely art – but art which must resist absolutely the temptation to invent. The least manipulation, the most modest re-arrangement of scene or sensation, and the contract between reader and documentarian is dead. As "Helen Demidenko" discovered, it is then too late to cry: "But this is fiction after all!"

Unlike fiction-writers, historians must keep their emotions bridled by intellect. It is because of that bridling that they have more chance than any novelist of penetrating sensibilities other than their own. The force of natural emotion is always difficult to resist. When I was reading the official records of the prolonged, expert torture sessions conducted within the institution we call the Spanish Inquisition, where every twist, every shriek, every moan was recorded, I read with brandy-and-water at my elbow to help me override my "emotions" long enough to get the task done – or until my "intellect" was too brandy-fuddled for me to continue. Why did I think that the task had to be done? Because it was essential to try to understand how humans could deliberately do such things to living human flesh. During that process of inquiry I believe my emotions were more powerfully and painfully implicated than any novelist's, because I had been drawn as close as it is now possible to get to a terrible past actuality.

Why do it? Because I believe it is useful in this world now.

Wislawa Szymborska has written a great poem titled, simply, "Tortures".

I cite only two (non-contiguous) verses. I beg you to find the time to read the whole:

> Nothing has changed.
> The body is susceptible to pain,
> it must eat and breathe air and sleep,
> it has thin skin and blood right underneath,
> an adequate stock of teeth and nails,
> its bones are breakable, its joints are stretchable.
> In tortures all this is taken into account ...
>
> Nothing has changed. Maybe just the manners, ceremonies, dances.
> Yet the movement of the hands in protecting the head is the same.
> The body writhes, jerks and tries to pull away,
> its legs give out, it falls, the knees fly up,
> it turns blue, swells, salivates and bleeds.
> Nothing has changed ...

A magnificent poem, with a weight of thought and experience behind it. But despite her experience, which utterly eclipses my own, I choose to believe Szymborska is wrong. My faith is that humans will injure each other less when they understand themselves and each other better. My task is to try to identify what it is in a particular situation which could make the obscene intimacies of torture possible. Therefore, the inquisition records. Anatomised, they might help me understand not only sixteenth-century Spain but Abu Ghraib, and how another Abu Ghraib might be prevented.

It might be true that humans are impervious to reason and compassion, and are therefore unredeemable. If they are, history is indeed "bunk", because its intrinsic purpose is to increase the role of reason and compassion in this world.

STORYTELLING AND HISTORY

Humans have a natural talent for stories. They are the only animal to make them, to tell them, to hoard them. They make stories in part because they need experience, their own and others, to be processed into a consultable form. This was clarified for me some years ago when by happy accident I heard the cognitive psychologist Jerome Bruner talk about a little girl called Emily. When Emily was about two, her parents noticed that she talked to herself, sometimes at length, after she had been put to bed. The little voice would start up, and it could go on for hours. Naturally the parents (who were also academics) wanted to know what their daughter was saying to herself in the privacy of her room. So they put a bug in her bed.

They discovered that Emily talked about many things. For example, she practised the past tense, which had been giving her trouble. But what she mainly did was make stories for herself out of what had happened that day: how she had dealt with it, how she might have dealt with it better; and this whether the happening was meeting a thug in the sandpit or reconciling herself to the cascading changes wrought by the arrival of a baby brother. The stories helped Emily make a moving picture of her infant world: to conceptualise and then to reflect on life situations so she could manage them more confidently, and at less psychological cost.

I think that is pretty much how the stories we tell ourselves in the privacy of our own heads work for us. But there is a problem, and we know it: our stories depend on memory, and memory is unreliable. We might bristle at any challenge, but at some point most of us begin to doubt. Are those shining childhood memories shards of bright experience, or were they made at second-hand from family photographs and family talk? A brother remembers a family drama with different words spoken, even different roles played; an ex-lover's memories deny ours at every point. But even as we wince at our memories' treachery, we cannot give them up. We need them for what Bruner calls "the rough and perpetually changing draft of our autobiography that we carry in our minds", which we can redraft with a vengeance should we feel the need: "I thought I married a prince; he was a frog who turned into a rat."

Our memories are essential; our memories are unreliable. Most of us live with that discomforting paradox. The serious social and political problems begin when stories cease to be personal possessions and come to be owned by a collectivity – a family, a club, a religion, an ethnicity, a nation-state. We can watch the first step of that progress from individual to group at any funeral and wake. Individuals offer up stories which are then selected, refined and integrated into what has become the agreed account of the deceased person, who is thus restored to a kind of social life, however diminished. There is comfort in that, but there is a cost, too. Henceforth stories which impugn the now-official account will have to be suppressed.

Collective stories have to be more dynamic than private ones because they have more work to do. They must represent the proper relationship within families, between genders, classes or nations, which in societies like ours, and nowadays everywhere else, are always changing. But once they have been sanctified as collective possessions, they must not appear to change. Custodians emerge: the family historian, the club's oldest member, the head of the local RSL. As the entities get larger, and the stakes get higher, de facto custodians must become official guardians of their particular bundle of collective memories, and find they have to invent crimes like blasphemy, heresy, treason or "being un-Australian" to see off any incubating counter-stories. Memorials and monuments designed to halt time by giving massive material form to especially sacred memories also change, as Ozymandias would have discovered if he had lived a few centuries longer. Memorials "memorialise" only for as long as people choose to remember.

Collective memories have many uses, only some of them benign. They might hold a beleaguered group together in the face of persecution, or keep a vision of a better future bright in the face of a dreadful present.

They might keep antique angers alive and dangerous, or sanctify conven-
ient customs to prolong corrupt rule or throttle debate. Historians stand
in a chronically tense relationship with such memory products, being at
once their preservers, and their unrelenting critics.

Occasionally there is an attempt to soften the terms of that relationship,
like the generous impulse, most visible in the new discipline of Subaltern
Studies, to award protected status to the collective memories cherished by
underdog groups. Respect for other people's stories is preferable to the
thick-headed arrogance which assumes the first story which leaps "to
mind" is the only possible one. There are also different ways of preserv-
ing the past. When Kwamchetsi Mamakoka tells us that "virtually all
Kikuyu claim to have belonged to the Mau Mau, regardless of whether
they were even alive in the 1950s," and goes on to remind us that Africans
love stories, that the stories are communally owned, that "it is not considered an abominable act of plagiarism to present another person's story
as your own," we learn something about Kikuyu we hadn't known before.
We are also reminded that stories work differently in different societies.
Equally, when we hear the stories British settlers were telling each other
during that same "uprising", we learn a lot we hadn't known before about
the British. But as the Kikuyu example makes clear, oral testimony is quite
as problematic as the written variety. Historians' scepticism must be universal. Nor do I accept that the cherished stories of a particular ethnic,
religious or national group have a truth-status equal or superior to post-
Enlightenment historians' criteria for evidence and probability. At a Mexi-
can museum, in delicate recognition of my Visiting Scholar status, I was
assigned their best "Aztec" guide. He was proud of his descent, and the
unstated premiss of all his fluent talk was "I am Aztec, so I know." He
didn't.

My personal conviction is that empirical critical history is not culture-
bound; that there are historians of the critical kind in every culture: individuals who hunger to know the real past rather than some consoling
mythicised version of it. Here I appeal to an important work of history

which in the clamour of the history wars was allowed to slide past almost unnoticed: Kim Scott and Hazel Brown's joint history of their Wilomin Noongar family, *Kayang and Me*. Scott had explored what it is to be of mixed descent in a casually racist Australia in his great novel *Benang*. Then he went into the archives to follow up some tantalising leads into his Aboriginal family history (he had been distanced but not divided from his mother's kin by his Scots father). Meanwhile his Wilomin aunt Hazel Brown, not yet known to him, was also reconstructing the family history, not from documents but from family stories: stories which she subjected to patient sifting and scrupulous testing. She cherished the stories. They were her family's only heritage. But she also knew their confusions, their evasions, their strategic silences. She wanted to know what had happened, and how the people involved, black and white, had thought and felt about it. What distinguished her from her nephew was not their passion for getting the history "right", but the mood in which they set about it. For Scott it was a finite task to be pursued and completed. Hazel Brown felt no such urgency. She trusted her research procedures. She trusted time to bring her new informants, as it had brought her nephew, laden with notes – littered with lacunae and errors – from the official archives. For Kayang Brown, this was not a professional project. She would be working on her family history for as long as she lived.

Stories are potent. They can rouse normally indolent people to action, as with asylum seekers and their supporters now struggling to bring their stories before the public while the Department of Immigration struggles to stifle or impugn them. But when people are using stories as weapons, they will simplify them, and with simplification a great deal can be lost. The "Stolen Generations" controversy was a war fought between stories. Which side was winning was indicated by the changes in the title which represented the evolving popular attitude. The report had been formally titled *Bringing them home: Report of the National Inquiry into the Separation of Aboriginal and Torres Strait Islander Children from Their Families*. With time and money short, the report had highlighted particularly painful stories: stories which quickly became iconic. The report's shorthand title became "The Stolen Generation Report", and then, in recognition of the duration of the child-removal policy, "The Stolen Generations Report". More recently the adjective has been recast as a verb: I read the other day about a woman "stolen when she was eight". No inverted commas. Nothing metaphorical about it at all. Interpretation has become mere description.

During that struggle, whole ideological stances would be inferred from whether commentators spoke of the children who had been the subjects of the inquiry as "stolen", or (more neutrally) "taken", or, as some hardliners insisted, "rescued". Meanwhile the stories-become-weapons were radically simplified by denuding them of their particular contexts. Unusually brutal abductions were presented as typical; the smudged thumb-print of an Aboriginal mother was taken as clear evidence of informed consent.

Now for one example of what was lost in that political process of strategic simplification. The "rescued" faction was delighted when under harsh interrogation Lowitja O'Donoghue, a distinguished Aboriginal spokeswoman, acknowledged she had not been "stolen", or even "taken". She had been given to a Catholic mission by her Irish father. Much triumphant right-wing chest-thumping: O'Donoghue had been "given", not "stolen"! Furthermore, she had clearly been rescued: look at her career! Even further more – if O'Donoghue hadn't been "stolen", perhaps hardly anyone, even no one, had?

Then the *Australian* newspaper sent O'Donoghue and the journalist Stuart Rintoul back to her birthplace to discover what had actually happened. They found that Lowitja had been two years old when she was taken from her tribal Aboriginal mother, Lily, and handed over by her father, along with two older siblings, to the mission; that her father had earlier given away two older children he had had with Lily; that this time he had kindly left her one infant still at the breast. Then when under a new law he had to choose between marrying Lily or taking a Carnal Knowledge rap, he grumpily paid his ten-shilling fine and costs and decamped to

Adelaide, where he married a white woman and become a pillar of white Catholic society.

This small, true story of Lowitja O'Donoghue's childhood is huge in its implications. It exposes the lying romance of "the frontier" by making us see just how vile that white masculine culture could be when gender inequality was joined to race: the criminal carelessness and casual brutality of some white men's dealings with indigenous people of this country. (Only "some". Other white men had readily, even eagerly married their Aboriginal wives.) As for the effect on Lowitja and her siblings: using Holocaust analogies for the "Stolen Children" experience has become something of a rhetorical habit among the activist Left. I dislike it, because, like all capacious comparisons, it blinds us to particularities. But on the issue of the immeasurability of long-term consequences, the parallel is just. We cannot measure the damage inflicted by a concentration-camp experience of two or three or five years' duration on the victim until the end of their life – or, indeed, of their children's lives. To do that we would have to know how the toxic residues of their suffering had been absorbed by neighbours, children, grandchildren. We also know that most of the children subjected to this drastic dislocation and "rehabilitation" were not accepted by white society, and that even those who have emerged as leaders – individuals, like Lowitja O'Donoghue, some whites want to count as unshadowed successes of the child-removal program – can only now acknowledge how deeply their removal injured them: that when they speak they are demanding justice not only for their silent brothers and sisters, but for their damaged selves.

Historians of whatever culture are at once the custodians of memory – the retrievers and preservers of the stories by which people have imagined their personal and civic lives – and the devoted critics of those stories. History wars over collective memories are fought everywhere, especially in national states with a significant degree of literacy and an organised education system. A fine brief statement of these complicated matters comes from David W. Blight, author of *Race and Reunion: The Civil War in American Memory*. Here is Blight on the differences between history and collective memory:

> History is what trained historians do, a reasoned reconstruction of the past rooted in research; it tends to be critical and skeptical of human motive and action, and therefore more secular than what people commonly call memory. History can be read by or belong to everyone; it is more relative, and contingent on place, chronology, and scale.
>
> If history is shared and secular, memory is often treated as a sacred set of absolute meanings and stories, possessed as the heritage or identity of a community. Memory is often owned, history interpreted. Memory is passed down through generations; history is revised. Memory often coalesces in objects, sites, and monuments; history seeks to understand contexts in all their complexity. History asserts the authority of academic training and canons of evidence; memory carries the often more immediate authority of community membership and experience ... historians study memory because it has been such an important modern instrument of power.

That recognition brings its own dilemma. The stories of suppressed groups can be re-animated to give people courage for a struggle towards justice. In such cases, ought historians hold their tongue? This is a genuinely difficult question, and individuals have answered and will answer it differently. My own sense is that the possible social and political consequences of elevating any bundle of memories to unchallengeable sacred status are simply too momentous and too unpredictable to allow that kind of restraint-from-criticism ordinance. However cherished, however jealously guarded, all human stories must be grist to the historian's mill — including, of course, our own.

Now hear Kate Darian-Smith, distinguished editor of a special issue of

Historical Studies titled "Challenging Histories" designed to find a new direction after the destructive muddle of the history wars:

> What is the role of history in the shaping of Australian identities? How can historians contribute to the future development of Australian society and culture? What are the responsibilities of the academic discipline of history in the wider processes of history-making within the public sphere in the twenty-first century? And how might knowledge of Australia's historical legacies influence and shape our responses to present social and political crises?

I think most historians in this country would find these formulations unexceptionable. I take a degree of exception to all of them, except, perhaps, the fourth. To begin with the third: it is true that in the relatively new branch of "history-making within the public sphere" – which includes working with newly vibrant museums – historians such as Graeme Davison have played essential and admirable parts. My anxieties centre on the academy's new economic circumstances. Nowadays professional historians are increasingly dependent on grants-based research, and subjected to the absurd requirement that projects should be pre-defined in terms of the social utility of their yet-to-be-found findings. As more public money comes to be spent on history, and with increasingly confining criteria claiming to measure utility and accountability being applied within the universities, the risk is that historians' primary responsibility will be understood to be to the present and the future of the nation and not to the past: that the true purpose of "Australian history" is patriotic and integrative. Add that to Australian historians' traditional role in "shaping the nation's destiny" and we are suddenly in deep waters.

Particular episodes from the national past have always been used, and will always be used, to serve mythic functions in the present. Not so very long ago "British History" was largely a treasure-house of nation-promoting stories, which is what we would expect from a glossy imperial power (compare the United States now). Most were about winners, but a few were about heroic losers like General Gordon, killed at Khartoum by the "Mad Mahdi" and his Arab rabble who ungratefully chose slavery, savagery and superstition over British civilisation and Christianity. Historians have since demonstrated that Gordon was significantly madder than the Mahdi, and that the "choices" before the Arabs did not include choice. In my view that is the historian's job: to unscramble what actually happened from whatever the current myth might be, and to inquire into what the myth-makers are up to – not to play at myth-making too.

Milan Kundera has famously declared that "the struggle of men against power is the struggle of memory against forgetting." That is well said. But precisely because memory as sacred relic functions as a dynamic agent in the present, its claims and uses must be kept under constant critical evaluation – as Ken Inglis did with his analysis of the manufacture of "Anzac Day", as Peter Cochrane did with "Simpson and the donkey", as Henry Reynolds did with his subversion of our self-congratulatory story of "the frontier".

Historians need to resist participating in the concoction of large, inspiriting narratives, because any large, inspiriting narrative requires significant narrowing of vision and manipulations of the truth. In this new century there has developed what I take to be an extension of the social power of history. Nowadays, in Elazar Barkan's aphorism, "History changes who we were, not just who we are." I think the "Who were we?" question is what the main fight has been about within Australian history these last years, and it seems to me (this might be idiosyncratic) a strange pursuit. I don't feel any special connection with my particular forebears. I do feel a connection to the country and to what has happened here, which manifests as an intensifying impulse to acknowledge past and present injustices, and to attempt restitution. But that impulse is now widespread, and it overleaps national boundaries. For example, it is expressed in the revived pursuit of an effective international court of justice and of effective international interventions where human rights are being scandalously abused. Supranational morality has never been popular with national governments. (Mr Howard has no desire to invade Guantánamo Bay.) Good history unconstrained by national boundaries has contributed to that widened quest for justice.

Within our own borders the moral implications of good history are most evident in the generation-long re-examination of Aboriginal–white relations since European settlement.

MORALITY IN HISTORY: HOW SORRY CAN WE BE?

In *Sense & Nonsense in Australian History*, John Hirst uses his essay "How Sorry Can We Be?" to declare his position on the moral implications of the history of race relations in this country. He begins by quoting Kipling's muscular response to a poem sent to him from Australia regretting "the bloody excesses of the empire's conquests". The imperial poet has no patience with what Hirst calls the "easy moralism" of the colonial poet, responding thus:

> A man might just as well accuse his father of a taste in fornication (citing his own birth as an instance) as a white man mourn over his land's savagery in the past.

Hirst:

> Let us label this the hard realist view of Australia's origins. It avers that it is morally impossible for settler Australians to regret or apologise for the conquest on which colonial Australia was built. It is a view I share.

It is also a view which, frankly, I do not understand, so both paragraph and quotation require a little analysis.

Kipling assigns "savagery" to "the land", not to the people contending for it. He frees the post-conquest white man from the fruitless business of "mourning". (It is unclear what emotional role he assigns to the conquered black, yellow, red or brown man, or woman either). Note too Hirst's yoking of the words "regret" and "apologise" as equally inappropriate, indeed impossible responses to the indubitable fact of conquest. I see these two words as indicating quite different moral situations: I can "regret" you got wet in the rain, but if you're wet because I tipped a bucket of water over you, surely I'd better apologise?

Or is Hirst saying it is logically impossible for us either to lament or to take any responsibility for the circumstances of our own creation?

Kipling's metaphor of the father "fornicating" – the sexual act unsanctioned by marriage – seems to suggest that. I am irresistibly reminded of Christopher Marlowe's exculpation of the Jew of Malta: "You have committed fornication/ but that was in another country/ and besides, the wench is dead." Kipling's view is that the child, the issue of the fornication, having had no voice in the business of his making, is born "clean". But what if the sex were not consensual? What if while happily "fornicating", that natural eruption of natural impulses, the father was also raping someone? How ought the fruit of that act of violence – whose father has given him every opportunity, whose mother has long been sent packing – feel, not only about his parents but also about his own present advantages? "Regret", surely? What else? Even "apology" seems a little inadequate. He might decide to seek out his abandoned mother to try to restore her to wellbeing and dignity. He might even be a little cool towards his genial, open-handed father. And we are back to the tedious business of measuring the nature, degree and duration of responsibility for the conquest which Hirst wants put behind us.

Was what happened in the contact zones of early Australia best described as "fornication", unsanctioned, true, but not too reprehensible, or was it rape? As always, a great deal hangs on the choice of metaphor, which distils argument into a word, and even more on locating an episode to ground discussion. I used to think the "rape" metaphor too harsh. My mind was changed by George Augustus Robinson on his 1841 journey as Protector of the Aborigines through colonial Victoria. Here is my single episode.

Robinson is in the territory of a man called Francis. Francis knows how to deal with blacks: if they cause him trouble – if they might cause him trouble – he shoots them. He is confident no action will be taken against him – "the authorities" are indolent, and too far away – and he is right. He tells Protector Robinson he has recently shot five men who had been disturbing his cattle, and another he found suspiciously close to the homestead sheepfold. He had ordered the station blacks (who were living and could only live on this white man's grace) to leave the body where it had fallen. Dogs had taken some of it, but the skull was still intact. Robinson picks up the skull and takes it away with him. As evidence? No. He is outraged by Francis's action, but he thinks nothing will be done about it. He has scientific interests. Perhaps he has taken the skull to put it into a collection.

This is how Robinson understands what is happening:

> Question: Where are the natives to go? the settlers or rather squatters do not allow the natives to stop at their home or out stations, then where are they to go? As many squatters claim for their runs from 2, 3 and 400 square miles of country, the home station and out stations, in many instances in a bad water country, secure all the water and the sheep and the cattle graze the intermediate space. Then where are the natives to go? ... are they to throw themselves in the mercy of other tribes because no British humanity exists in the hearts of British Australian squatters towards the original occupants of the soil?

In 1841 Robinson knew there were choices being made, and that different choices could have been made. Granted, those "squatters" – those white men who had seized the land and the water and ejected or subjugated the original inhabitants – were not going to leave. That makes the question: how could their cruelty have been prevented or, more realistically, mitigated? What could "British humanity" – in which Robinson, despite experience, still believes – have done? That is an historical question, but it is also a moral one. Daily we enjoy the fruits of what those hard men did. Our present comforts derive from their past actions. If Hirst believes we have no responsibility and therefore no obligations arising from whatever occurred before our nation's birth (I could well have him wrong here, but that is what his words say to me), when does our nation's responsibility for the past begin? Not at birth: Hirst's vision gives no place to original sin. At eight? At ten? At sixteen? When? More important: granted that the Aborigines would be driven off or to the periphery of their land, surely the degree and the style of the violence matters: whether it is brutal, casual, careless or remorseful. I am glad this continent was not "discovered" by Spaniards in the sixteenth century, because they would have shed much more blood than did the British of the late eighteenth century. The Spaniards were reckless in such matters. The British were not. But both native groups were finally "conquered". Does that make distinction and comparison irrelevant?

Later in the essay Hirst develops a distinction between what he identifies as the two main periods of Aboriginal affliction at the hands of the white men. The first "attack" was the initial conquest, the second the official thrust from 1900 on "to control, confine and manage Aborigines", including the policies of child-removal, in the interest of keeping Australia white. (The period between Hirst surprisingly identifies as "a laissez-faire time". "Laissez-faire" for whom?) Hirst argues there can be no apology for the first attack: the conquest. Why not? Because that first offence was committed not by "Australians", but by "the settlers … English, Irish and Scots who invaded Aboriginal lands with the sanction of the British state. Only subsequently was the Australian nation formed by those settlers and their children." The nation made possible by that expropriation is not implicated in the injury, therefore the nation cannot apologise. By contrast, "the second attack was an attack by the Australian nation … in pursuit of a national ideal."

This seems to be a strangely legalistic argument depending on remarkably crisp periodisation. When did this "Australian nation" come into being? I can suggest several dates, all of them arbitrary. What are we to do about the continuity of personnel? How are we to regard a man who on Friday is an Irishman and on Saturday is an Australian? Does being born in "Australia" bring responsibility for the nation's actions with it? How is "a nation" actualised? In its government? If Benedict Anderson is right, and "the nation" is an imagined community, how many of its members would be required to endorse the apology before it became real? I admit I am baffled by this. I have the sense of missing the point.

Hirst then goes on to a further distinction: the different degrees of moral opprobrium we ought to allocate to what Hirst describes as "hot-blooded" acts, and to "cold-blooded" acts. Hirst:

> I am not shocked at a settler riding out to shoot Aborigines. He acted in hot blood to protect what was close to him, the lives of himself and his workers and the survival of his highly risky enterprise. Nor am I shocked that settlers and their men sometimes rode out together hoping to kill enough Aborigines to give them finally the security they craved. But I cannot be calm at police arriving at settled communities to drag children away from their mothers. This was cold-blooded cruelty planned by a distant Bureau in pursuit of the ideal of racial purity.

He also believes that "cruelty of this sort did not appear until the early twentieth century."

To begin with the last: it is difficult to recall a more bureaucratised cruelty than that exercised, with chilling dispassion, by the Spanish Inquisition. Humans have always been good at cruelty. What interests me more is Hirst's evaluation of acts in terms of his own emotional response ("shocked" or "not shocked"), and the authority he is according his own estimate of the blood-temperatures of those committing acts he presumably acknowledges to be reprehensible. Was Francis "act[ing] in hot blood to protect what was close to him, the lives of himself and his workers and the survival of his highly risky enterprise" when he shot the man spotted by his sheepfold, or was this a casual murder committed as a reflex of a grossly inflated notion of "squatters' rights" over a despised people? The occasional shooting of blacks by whites in sport has been sufficiently well established as historical fact. How "hot-blooded" was that?

It is possible that nearly as many Aborigines would have died of misery, hunger and disease without the deliberate killings. But surely it is a crucial part of the historian's duty to uncover how it was that some settlers were killers, and others were not? It is only by establishing the span of choices open to these men that we can hope to understand why individuals made the choices they did.

Hirst believes "there is literally no place for settler Australians to stand to decry the conquest of this country." But we are not only "settler Australians". We are moral beings as well. In my view historians have a special responsibility to examine the actions of men and women, in this case men and women who happen to be our predecessors, to discover what choices they had, what choices they made, and how we are to understand those choices.

Hirst was provoked to write this essay, "How Sorry Can We Be?", by his accumulating irritation with what he calls the "liberal fantasy" that the conquest – the taking of this land for our own purposes, which were incompatible with Aboriginal purposes – could have been "done nicely". I think few people who have engaged seriously with the history of this country think that – except, possibly, Keith Windschuttle, who seems to think it was done as nicely as it possibly could be.

His irritation was distilled when in the superheated air of a writers' festival session, after a protracted discussion about numbers and what counts as evidence, a woman declared that "even one [Aboriginal] death was one too many." Hirst took this remark to be a soft-headed expression of "the liberal fantasy view of our origins". Was she really expressing a view about history, or was this a moment of moral and emotional revulsion, standing close to Hirst's own revulsion from what was done during the period of the child-removal policy? Surely there, at the level of moral evaluation, he would judge one screaming child, one desperate mother, to be "too many"?

Agreed, it is futile to wring our hands over past brutalities and injustices, but we can seek to analyse them with sufficient delicacy to understand how it was that some individuals chose to commit brutal acts, and that others, in similar circumstances, did not; to examine how our fathers or any humans could entertain so narrowed a notion of humanity, so restricted a view of situation and choice, that they could inflict lethal injury so readily. We would then be better able to count the cost of our present comfort, and not take it as a gift of nature or (worse) as our natural due. We might even choose to try to alleviate those acts' most damaging legacies.

I also quarrel with Hirst's neat periodisation. In this country the process of conquest, including the spilling of blood, cannot be penned within a narrowly defined pre-national period. It has gone on for a very long time. Expropriation has gone on even longer. The anthropologist Frances Morphy informs us that many Arnhemlanders think that whites owe them a living. Why? Because we snatched their land and their living away from them only yesterday.

Hirst's essay pivots on the issue of the proper relationship between history and morality. He is against moralising; so am I. Historians ought not preach because preaching is both tedious and unilluminating. A young historian employs most of the preface to her book about slavery in the United States to reassure me she is "against slavery". I don't much care whether she is or not. What I want to know is whether she can help me understand how such a system could have survived so long in a society which employed the rhetoric of liberty and where interracial contact was often prolonged and intimate. I also want to know what slave-holders, slave-traders and slaves thought about that system in its several variations: how they tried to exploit, accommodate, modify or escape from it. When I was writing about Aztecs, ought I have added: "By the way, I disapprove of human sacrifice, especially the strangling of babies"? As it happens I do, but my task was to show how it was that Aztecs accepted the necessity of the ritualised killing of humans, including the strangling of terrified toddlers, in a society which cherished its children.

Nonetheless ... doing history is a lonely business, and the energy for it has to come from somewhere. Historians will research and write about what they most care about. If they didn't (when they don't), they write dull history which will probably also be bad history. But what they most care about sets only the initial question: "What happened to women-at-home during the First World War?" "What happened to Aborigines when the white men came?" "When did British workers begin to think in terms of class?" The chosen question might have more to do with personal history than moral/political attitudes, if they can ever be separated. For me, growing up in a household with "The War" a brooding presence, the infliction of taken-for-granted, deliberate violence on fellow humans became the great conundrum. But while such impulses, conscious or less than conscious, will influence the choice of topic and the initial question, they must not be allowed to influence the findings.

If it is condescending to preach morality, smug to assume agreement and mawkish to display one's own sensibility, how can the historian's moral vision be manifested? Sometimes directly, as when E.P. Thompson nails his colours to the mast (see later in this essay). Sometimes discreetly, as when Christopher Browning, in my view the best Anglo historian of the Holocaust, reconstructs the daily activities of the Nazi administration of the Occupied Territory of Poland. Browning dispassionately presents the sequence of increasingly punitive "administrative orders" made against Jews. He shows us those orders being contested within the cross-currents of individual and factional ambition, ideological zeal and the ardent pursuit of Hitler's flighty favour. "Office politics", we might call it. Then Browning drops one word into that carefully dispassionate account. He names these preoccupied bureaucrats "murderers". That single word does two things. It jolts us back to full awareness of the horror of what these men were doing, and we glimpse the moral rage behind Browning's dispassion.

The most assured historians reveal their moral vision in everything they do: through tone, the sequencing of topics, the interspersion of comment, the selection of particular moments for deeper inquiry. That is why my most engrossing aesthetic/intellectual pleasure from words on the page, excepting only poetry, comes from watching a master historian at work. It is a preposterously ambitious enterprise, trying to make whole

people, whole situations, whole other ways of being out of the dusty frag-
ments left after real lives end, but that is what the best historians set out
to do. Their core narrative is always their struggle with recalcitrant, evasive sources. As they interrogate those sources before our eyes, we have a
fleeting sense of what it would have been like to have lived a different life,
in a different place, at a different time.

If all this makes the writing of history sound like an advanced literary
art, so, of course, it is.

Nearly thirty years ago Henry Reynolds declared both his principles and
his purposes before an audience of academic historians:

> The work of the historian cannot be sealed off from the community
> … History should not only be relevant but politically utilitarian …
> It should aim to right old injustices, to discriminate in favour of the
> oppressed, to actively rally to the cause of liberation.

Doubtless some of those listening said then, as some still say: "Prepos-
terous! Whatever happened to objectivity?" Nothing has happened to
objectivity. Reynolds has made the occasional error; when they have been
pointed out, he has corrected them. He has also had a triumph not commonly granted historians: his research has informed major judicial deci-
sions. He has done this, and could only have done this, by maintaining
the strict rules of the discipline over years of intricate research. He is the
closest thing this country has produced to the man I take to be the greatest historian of eighteenth-century British social and political history – a
history of immense consequence to Australia, giving us our law and the
vision of a secular liberal democracy compatible with social justice.

In the preface to his *The Making of The English Working Class*, in what has
become a "light on the hill" passage among historians, E.P. Thompson
explains why he does what he does:

> I am seeking to rescue the poor stockinger, the Luddite cropper, the
> 'obsolete' hand-loom weaver, the 'Utopian' artisan, and even the

deluded follower of Joanna Southcott, from the enormous conde-
scension of posterity. Their crafts and traditions may have been
dying. Their hostility to the new industrialism may have been back-
ward-looking. Their communitarian ideals may have been fantasies.
Their insurrectionary conspiracies may have been foolhardy. But
they lived through these times of acute social disturbance, and we
did not ... Our only criterion of judgement should not be whether
or not a man's actions are justified in the light of subsequent evolution. After all, we are not at the end of social evolution ourselves.

Then comes the forward view:

In some of the lost causes of the people of the Industrial Revolution
we may discover insights into social evils which we have yet to
cure. Moreover, the greater part of the world today is still undergo-
ing problems of industrialization, and of the formation of democratic
institutions, analogous in many ways to our own experience during
the Industrial Revolution.

And then, at the last, comes the political aspiration, kept fastidiously
separate from the history:

Causes which were lost in England might, in Asia or Africa, yet be
won.

Thompson's appetite for work was gargantuan. He was so passionate a
researcher as to make Keith Windschuttle look like a dabbler. He had to
duck-dive again and again through the rhetorical extravagances of the
ruling caste of the late eighteenth and early nineteenth century to retrieve
the counter-stories being told by the people who were in process of being
processed into a working class. Their voices were hard to hear, and it took
an historian of genius to hear them. But through Thompson's work those
voices have been discovered, preserved and made accessible to the rest of
us: part of the great reservoir of human experience we call "the past".

THE HISTORY PROJECT

Given that we need informed patriotism, how are we to create and nurture new nation-unifying experiences? I doubt Mr Howard's campaign for orchestrated flag-worship will do it, not least because Australians are free from the terrifying piety of that model patriotic society, heartland America. In America, flags sprout everywhere, as if, in Guy Rundle's words, "there were some doubt as to the sovereignty of this particular apartment or that news-stand." There are flags on cars, along with declamatory bumper stickers, most of them reassuring the pursuing driver of the "saved" state of the motorist's soul. Few are sensitive to history, so I was unreasonably cheered by the sticker on a beaten-up yellow Cadillac sighted in Austin, Texas: "You might have come across in the *Mayflower*, but your daughter came across in here." Excerpts from the approved national history narrative litter the landscape. At a university town in Oregon we were put up at a famous "historic house", which turned out to be four years younger than my husband. It looked much older, with its fake lamps with little pull-chain switches, the lumpy patchwork quilt on the four-poster bed with the painting of stage-coachers fighting off Indians suspended over it. There are History Theme Parks galore, with cheerful hostesses in various "historic" outfits happy to pose for photographs, but the theme is always the same: "This Land was Made for You and Me". Made by whom? God, of course. For American Indians? African-Americans? Mexican-Americans? Hell no. For Us.

That style of patriotic "history" induces the belligerent exceptionalism we are watching now. It also sustains a frightening ignorance about how the United States is viewed by the rest of the world. This corrupt, feel-good "history" — tirelessly taught in the schools — has not served the United States well. It is essential that we avoid it here.

Which I think we will manage rather easily. As the immortal Don Marquis said, you don't have to have a soul unless you really want one, and I don't think most Australians do. Despite scattered eruptions of religious zeal, we remain a comfortably secular society. As for those federally funded flagpoles: I doubt Australian schoolchildren will imbibe patriotic virtue through being made to line up to salute the flag. I think that belief is grounded in an ageing man's nostalgia for his childhood, when the world was a sweeter place. But I was there, too, and I used the flag ceremony to practise rebellion. Every Monday morning I was told to put my hand on my heart and recite: "I love God and my country, I honour the Crown, and cheerfully obey my parents, teachers and the law"; every Monday morning I objected to being made to tell lies.

While I didn't love God, didn't honour the Crown, didn't cheerfully obey my teachers and parents (as yet I had had no problem with the law), I had not doubt I loved my country. I loved it for its physical being, above all its beaches, but also because I knew something of its history, through public celebrations like Anzac Day and also through stories from my family history. Coming from a working-class background, I was very aware of the triumphs of the trade union movement here. I knew that, unlike England, Australia was a land of opportunity, with class divisions porous for people of courage and tenacity. My father and his father before him had proved it. I was consciously proud of that, just as I was proud of every single member of our cricket team along with Phar Lap and Ned Kelly.

It was a sturdy nationalism, acquired early, lasting long, but it became conscious and systematised only through a later experience, when I discovered how Australia manages the difficult business of allocating human organs for transplantation. Australia is one of the few countries where organ transplantation is done only in public hospitals. You can't buy yourself a heart or a liver or a set of lungs in Australia, and you can't buy your way to the top of the queue. The distribution of these tragically scarce resources is strictly egalitarian. Donor families are not paid, and remain anonymous. They choose, in a time of anguish, to make their gift to any fellow citizen. At the same time I got to know a big public hospital, and saw the success of our immigration program at first-hand, as a range of cultural sensibilities were treated with humour and tenderness by a marvellously multicultural staff.

Given that my own loyalty – my steady preference for this country above all others – comes out of decades of personal experience, I do not think we can make a prior demand for incomers to be "loyal" to the past or even the present of this nation. They have been shaped by different histories, different experiences. However, I think we can reasonably expect newcomers to learn enough of Australia's political development to be aware of its distinctive features: to accept that secular democracy is its political system, with no place for the imposition of a religious vision under the direction of priests. Such a vision may be pursued, but within the zone of the personal, not the political. But if each of us makes our own Australia out of personal experience, so generating patriotism of the only reliable kind, we can hope that with luck, generosity and careful planning recent arrivals can be helped to their own moments of success and happiness, and so to pride in "being Australian".

This is to ask a lot. Incomers face enough challenges, trying to find work, struggling to learn enough English to find a secure place in this society. It will be the children who matter most, so Mr Howard is right. Schools will be where the action is – which is where it has been for the last twenty and more years. I liked the Prime Minister's suggestion in his Australia Day speech that the history of immigration be taught, so each group will be able to locate itself – "this is where we came from, this is when we came and where we went, these were our problems" – while learning that other groups went through similar experiences. I liked even more his suggestion that indigenous history provide a foundation stone for what came later. I have nothing against Simpson and his donkey being a story for telling and reflecting on in primary school, provided it is thought about analytically and critically in secondary school. But can values be taught by way of reformed history curricula? That seems to me doubtful. Do I think the curricula ought be "reformed" by some ardent "Coalition of the Willing"? Heaven forbid. I can imagine altogether too easily who would be the most willing. (I wrote this before I was invited to attend the History Summit. My view stands.)

In special circumstances, values can sometimes be taught through exhortation – provided the exhortation is accompanied by energetic action. Chris Sarra, one-time head of the apparently terminally demoralised state school at Cherbourg, gives a thrilling account of the policies and practices he used to transform the experience and the performance of his students in the space of a handful of years. Values are always best taught by action. A couple of decades ago a friend of mine was teaching the Infant Class at Richmond West Primary School in Melbourne. The school stood in the long shadow of the Housing Commission flats, so year by year wave after wave of little kids arrived with little or no English, and some with no experience of school at all. My friend had to revise her teaching strategies accordingly. In the first class of the year she would lie down on the floor and draw her outline in chalk (which, when you think about it, is quite a feat), and then name the parts. When the time came to teach arithmetic, she did it by way of an intensive study of the AFL football scores, and that worked, too. This was Richmond, after all.

I think her unselfconscious, do-it-yourself strategies must have taught those anxious children a great deal about "Australian values". Here was a teacher so confident of her authority, and so serious about what she was doing, that she would lie down on the floor to do it: who got her lessons across by vivid engagement and laughter. I would like to think these are "core Australian values" in action. For those children the initial bewilderment, then the laughter, made them into a little society, which could begin to locate itself within the wider neighbourhood. (This is what I have against "faith" schools. They take children out of their neighbourhoods and ghettoise them.)

I don't think the Prime Minister can have his pride-generating "objective record of achievement" either, because there can be no purely objective record of achievement of anything as complicated as a nation. Such a history would too easily become a guided tour of the elevating bits of the nation's past. A less guided tour would have to reveal, for example, just how exclusivist this "nation" has been from its beginning, with convicts not belonging to it, then the Irish not belonging until they had served a long apprenticeship. The West Indian blacks and the American Indians arriving with the first fleets did not belong to it, nor did the Chinese or the Afghans who came later. Australian Aborigines have never belonged to it, because there is no easy way to fit them into a triumphalist narrative. Serious history subverts such covert exclusivism, as it subverts other strategic deformations of "what happened". It also makes us better able to appreciate the remarkable open-heartedness displayed by large sections of the population towards incomers.

I would like students at every level to study Australian history because I believe that one of the best ways to "teach values" is to exercise minds by engaging them in investigation of conflicts between competing values and interests, always with a proper regard for clarity and justice of analysis and the relevance of evidence. As for the details of curricula and lesson plans: as my teacher brother tirelessly reminds me, I have never had to face a class of fifteen-year-olds just back from the summer break. Teachers must play the major part in devising the history curriculum for the different levels, because only they face the new breed of teenager and know what is practicable.

Nonetheless, I hope they will canvas opinion widely. My first request is practical. I would like to see the distribution of a complex time-line − a time-line which includes major events elsewhere − so that students can see how the local episodes they are burrowing into relate, or seem not to relate, to events elsewhere. Governor Phillip, struggling to keep his remote little colony afloat, heard about the French Revolution only long after it had happened. That knowledge jolts us, accustomed to a world of instant communication, into awareness of the terrifying isolation in which Phillip was making his grand experiment in inter-cultural harmony. The mapping of major events elsewhere might also reduce our pronounced tendency towards parochialism.

My second request focuses on "essential" political content. Does it matter that schoolchildren don't know the name of the first Australian prime minister? I didn't know it myself until it suddenly became a test of citizenship, and I still know nothing at all about the man. The Minister for Education, Julie Bishop, was shocked that when students were asked to name a political leader of this country who was famous in the period 1880–1901, most were unable to name one, while among the names suggested by those game enough to try were "Arthur Phillip, Menzies and Ronald Reagan". But why should they know the name of "a political leader … who was famous in the period 1880–1901", and not about the shearers' strike of 1891 or the agricultural depression which provoked it? Or, for that matter, about Australia's involvement in the Boer War? I cannot see the utility of elevating a local political narrative over enquiry into major social movements or international engagements.

I do, however, see some "political history" as essential to our national sense of self. Consider the confident talk not so long ago about "democracy", meaning our kind of democracy, "taking root", even "flowering", in the alien soils of Iraq and Afghanistan. We no longer believe that. Meanwhile the rule of law is proving to be more vulnerable than we had thought. Evidence? Look at the United States of America and the extraordinary expansion of executive power. Look at some disquieting "developments" here. Our liberal, secular democracy turns out to be not the highway for humanity but a particular road dependent on particular historical contingencies, with all that implies about chronic vulnerability. We therefore urgently need to understand how it was brought into being, and to identify its peculiar characteristics and vulnerabilities.

The British historian Lawrence Stone brings the relevant questions into crisp focus:

> … how and why did Western Europe change itself during the sixteenth and eighteenth centuries so as to lay the social, economic, political, ideological and ethical foundations for the rationalist,

democratic, individualistic, technological industrialised society in which we now live?

Stone goes on to trace how that path has been travelled by Western European nation-states, each in its own fashion. French democracy is differently flavoured from the British, with a heavier emphasis on equality; American democracy is its own peculiar blend; ours is different again.

I would like school-leavers to have a broad understanding of that slice of European history because it is crucial to our future, and also because the vision which animated it is increasingly under threat. Notions of progress based on technological advances have also been taking a beating lately. The twentieth century was the bloodiest century in human history, largely because humans added technologised war to more traditional techniques of killing other humans. During that century we came to accept, with truly astonishing alacrity, the deaths of hundreds of thousands of non-combatant civilians in national conflicts as a tolerable price to pay for uncertain political outcomes. In this century overt colonialism might be in eclipse, but covert imperialism is proving to be at least as corrosive and significantly more irresponsible. Meanwhile improved military technology has shifted the human costs of war away from well-equipped soldiers onto notably less well-equipped enemy combatants, as in the First Gulf War, and then on to "enemy" civilians, as happened during the Second Iraq War, as is happening now in Lebanon. This is the strange and bitter fruit of "progress".

We live in a global economy, but not a global polity. We have global terrorists, but no effective global government. While global capitalism flourishes, inequalities between classes and peoples widen. Meanwhile the poor have become both more mobile and less resigned. We no longer have the option of living snugly behind our borders, ignoring the desperate people outside.

Some people think history is useless because change is so swift. It is precisely because change is so swift that we need history. This new century brings a new urgency to the historian's task. Under the onslaught of commercial trivia, and with the growing assumption that only the individual and the individual story has meaning ("there is no society"), the faculty of memory might itself be eroding. From Eric Hobsbawm's *The Age of Extremes*:

> The destruction of the past ... is one of the most eerie phenomena of the late twentieth century. Most young men and women at the century's end grow up in a sort of permanent present lacking any organic relation to the public past of the times they live in.

I hope Hobsbawm is wrong. Nonetheless, we must act as if he were right.

Who owns the past? In a free society, everyone. It is a magic pudding belonging to anyone who wants to cut themselves a slice, from legend-manufacturers through novelists looking for ready-made plots, to interest groups out to extend their influence. Well-told stories about the past can have large consequences. A powerful story might elicit remorse in a dominant group, and even stimulate the desire to recompense injury. At least as often stories can be used to create or to consolidate hatreds, whether by commission, like the "revised" history of India recently contrived by fundamentalist Hindus with Indian Muslims cast as barbaric invaders, or by omission, as in Japan's obstinate amnesia regarding what its armies did in China.

Given the power of stories, historians must be on constant alert regarding their uses, because, like their cousins the archaeologists, their obligation is to preserve the past in its least corrupted form. Citizens will go on exploiting the past for all manner of private and public enterprises, reputable and disreputable; historians will go on resisting opportunistic appropriations. That critical role will engage them in "politics" broadly understood. Here I quote myself from the good old days when we had the *Australian's Review of Books* and Luke Slattery was its editor:

History in the grand narrative sense will always belong to the victors, whether the war is between peoples, or classes, or genders, or generations. They will create and control the official record, and their point of view will inform the stories which present themselves as no more than innocent, "objective" descriptions of "what happened". If we are to learn anything useful from the great human resource of past experience, we have to begin by destabilising those self-congratulatory accounts of the past, because the past, like the present, is simply too complicated and too multiple to be told in any single story.

Through the anatomising of past situations we can hope to increase our ability to recognise what choices were available to men and women in past situations, however coercive those situations might have appeared to be. When we have done that, we might be better able to identify the real choices before us now, and not succumb to externally imposed notions of "responsibility" and "necessity". We have to know the world as it is if we are to change any part of it, and to map the span for human agency so we do not acquiesce in what we could change. Good history might also help us count the cost of inflicting present pain in the expectation of uncertain future benefits. It might even dispel our chronic amnesia regarding war.

How are historians to do any of these things, much less all of them, when their chosen "field" includes anything and everything produced by human minds? I think they must cultivate the quality John Keats identified in William Shakespeare:

At once it struck me, what quality went to form a man of Achievement especially in Literature & which Shakespeare possessed so enormously – I mean Negative Capability, that is when man is capable of being in uncertainties, Mysteries, doubts, without any irritable reaching after fact & reason ...

"Negative capability". The ability to watch patiently, through time, with steady, even attentiveness: to resist the rush to interpretation. Bertrand Russell:

> To endure uncertainty is difficult, but so are most of the other virtues. For the learning of every virtue there is an appropriate discipline, and for the learning of suspended judgement the best discipline is philosophy.

Russell might be right, but in my view History runs Philosophy a very close second.

To embrace uncertainty and ambiguity is the historian's special duty. But if history is to inform present choices – to make them both more intelligent and more compassionate, as I believe it can – it must abide by the iron rules of the discipline.

As for "good historical methods", so difficult to describe, so recognisable in action – hear Charles Darwin reflecting on the character and movement of his intellectual life in the last section of his autobiography:

> I have no great quickness of apprehension or wit which is so often remarkable in some clever men ... My power to follow a long and purely abstract train of thought is very limited. My industry has been nearly as great as it could have been in the observation and collection of facts ... From my early youth I have had the strongest desire to understand or explain whatever I observed [in nature] ... These causes combined have given me the patience to reflect or ponder for any number of years over any unexplained problem.

Now hear E.P. Thompson explain the transformative power of this passionate empiricism:

> From their base in 'second causes' the natural sciences were massing against the First Cause itself, or if not against God ... then against magical notations of the origin of the natural world and of

man. Biology, geology, natural history, astronomy, after decades of empirical accumulation – all were pressing matters to a decision. And the break-through, the moment of synthesis, came, not with some English Voltaire immersed in metropolitan tumult, but with a neurotic, secluded, intellectually evasive man, once destined for a clerical career, who nevertheless was a protagonist of an inherited empirical habit, which was raised in him to a pitch of intensity, until it became a breathtaking intellectual courage, as he laboriously restructured whole sciences and effected a new synthesis. We cannot come away from any account of Darwin without the conviction that a respect for fact is not only a technique, it can also be an intellectual force in its own right.

This seems to me a fair account of how devotion to intelligent observation can transform understanding. Historians share Darwin's credo, from *The Descent of Man*: "We are not here concerned with hopes and fears, only with truth as far as our reason allows us to discover it." I would like them to take their epitaph, much less modest than it sounds, from Darwin too: "I have given the evidence to the best of my ability."

Inga Clendinnen, 7 August 2006

POSTSCRIPT

This manuscript goes to the publisher today. In a few days' time I will be attending the History Summit on the reformation of the teaching of Australian history in schools called by the federal Education Minister, Julie Bishop.

I go with several hopes. One is that practising history teachers will be in control of the translation into teaching action of whatever "structure of facts, dates and events" the group recommends. Another is that whatever narrative might be constructed out of agreed "facts, dates and events", that process will be recognised as the exercise in selection and interpretation it is, and be open to systematic critical evaluation. I also hope it will be acknowledged that given the multiplicity of possible perspectives, there can be no purely "objective record of achievement" of anything as complicated as a nation. And last: that history's social utility depends on it being cherished as a critical discipline, and not as a tempting source of gratifying tales.

Wish me luck.

SOURCES

1   John Howard, Address to the National Press Club, Great Hall, Parliament House, 25 January 2006, <http://www.pm.gov.au/news/speeches/speech 1754.html>.

8   Amanda Lohrey, *Quarterly Essay 22: Voting for Jesus*, Black Inc., Melbourne, 2006, p.37.

8-9   Mark McKenna, "Writing the Past", <www.humanitieswritingproject.net. au/mckenna.htm>. The lecture also appeared in the *Australian Financial Review*, 16 December 2005. Also see the penetrating discussion in Ann Curthoys and John Docker, *Is History Fiction?*, UNSW Press, Sydney, 2005.

10   Simpson and his donkey: as it happens, much of the necessary historical work has already been done by a historian named Peter Cochrane, in a book called *Simpson and the Donkey: The Making of a Legend*, Melbourne University Press, Carlton, 1992.

10   Ken Inglis, *Sacred Places: War Memorials in the Australian Landscape*, Miegunyah Press at Melbourne University Press, Carlton, 1998, especially Ch. 9, "Australia Remembers".

13   Humphrey McQueen, "Gallipoli's Shadows", *The Age*, 25 April 2003.

15   "Australian historians have done fine work on Anzac Day": as well as the contributions by McKenna, Inglis and McQueen, see also Bruce Scates and Raelene Frances, *Women and the Great War*, Cambridge University Press, Cambridge, 1998, esp. Ch. 5, "Loss, Bereavement and Remembrance". And for a wider view of a universal phenomenon, see James E. Young (ed.), *Holocaust Memorials in History: The Art of Memory*, Prestel Verlag, New York, 1994.

16   "novelists have been doing their best to bump historians off the track": for an overview of these ambitions see Mark McKenna, op. cit.

16-17   "Challenging Australian History: discovering new narratives", a seminar held at the National Library in Canberra on 14–15 April 2000. See <www. nla.gov.au/events/history>. You will find Grenville's paper at <www.nla. gov.au/events/history/papers/Kate_Grenville%20.html>.

17-20, 24 Kate Grenville interviewed by Ramona Koval on ABC Radio National, "Books and Writing", 8 January 2006, <www.abc.net.au/rn/arts/bwriting/stories/ s1527708.htm>.

18   "the critiques of John Hirst and Mark McKenna": McKenna, op. cit.; and John Hirst, "How Sorry Can We Be?", in *Sense & Nonsense in Australian History*, Black Inc., Melbourne, 2006.

23   Michelle Z. Rosaldo, *Knowledge and Passion: Ilongot Notions of Self and Social Life*, Cambridge University Press, Cambridge, 1980.

24-5   Ralph Clark, *The Journal and Letters of Lt. Ralph Clark 1787–1792*, edited by Paul G. Fidlon and R.J. Ryan, Australian Documents Library in association with the Library of Australian History, Sydney, 1981.

27   Louis O. Mink "The Autonomy of Historical Understanding", *History and Theory*, 5:1 (1966) 24–47, p.42.

28   Henry James to Sarah Orne Jewett, 5 October 1901, *Henry James, Letters*, edited by Leon Edel, The Belnap Press, Cambridge, Mass., 1984, vol. iv, pp.208–9. The capitals and italics are, of course, his.

30   Don Watson, *Caledonia Australis: Scottish Highlanders on the Frontier of Australia*, Vintage, Milsons Point, 1984, 1997.

32   Peter Carey, *Australian Book Review*, Dec/Jan 1997, p.18.

33   Vladimir Nabokov, *Lectures on Russian Literature*, edited and introduced by Fredson Bowers, Harcourt Brace, NY/London, 1981, p.213.

34   Philip Roth, *Reading Myself and Others*, Penguin, Harmondsworth, 1985, p.120.

35   Kate Jennings, "Among the strong and the shrewd", *Australian Financial Review*, 1 May 2003.

37   Wislawa Szymborska, "Tortures", *View with a Grain of Sand: Selected Poems*, Harvest Books, Orlando, Florida, 1995.

38   You can read about Emily and what various academic tribes made of her, including a surprisingly dull essay by Bruner, in *Narratives from the Crib*, edited by Karen Nelson, Harvard University Press, Cambridge, Mass., 1989.

38-9   "the rough and perpetually changing draft": Jerome Bruner, *Acts of Meaning*, Harvard University Press, Cambridge, Mass., 1990, p.33.

40   Kikuyu and British: Caroline Elkins, *Britain's Gulag: The Brutal End of Empire in Kenya*, Jonathan Cape, London, 2005.

41   Kim Scott and Hazel Brown, *Kayang and Me*, Fremantle Arts Press, Fremantle, 2005.

42   "The 'rescued' faction was delighted": Andrew Bolt, "I Wasn't Stolen", *Herald Sun*, 23 February 2000.

42   "Then the *Australian* newspaper sent O'Donoghue": Stuart Rintoul, "Going Home", *The Weekend Australian Magazine*, 21–22 April 2001.

44   David W. Blight, "Historians and 'Memory'", <www.common-place.org>, vol. 2, no. 3, April 2002. See also his *Race and Reunion: The Civil War in American Memory*, Harvard University Press, Cambridge, Mass., 2001.

45   Kate Darian-Smith, introduction to "Challenging Histories: Rereading the Past", Special Issue, *Australian Historical Studies*, 33:118, 2002.

48   Hirst, op. cit., p.80.

49-50   George Augustus Robinson: *Journals of G.A. Robinson, May to August 1841*, edited with an introduction by Gary Presland, Records of the Victorian Archeological Society, no. 11, 1980, pp.125–127.

51-2   Hirst, op. cit., pp.90-1.

53   Hirst, op. cit., pp.82.

56-7   Henry Reynolds quoted in Mark McKenna, *Looking for Blackfellas' Point: an Australian History of Place*, UNSW Press, Sydney, 2002, p.46.

56   E.P. Thompson, *The Making of the English Working Class*, Penguin Books, Harmondsworth, 1963, 1968, p.12.

58   Guy Rundle, "Flagging Passions", *The Age*, 1 April 2006.

61   Chris Sarra, "Armed for Success", *Getting Smart, Griffith Review*, Autumn 2006.

63-4   Lawrence Stone, *The Past and the Present Revisited*, Routledge, London, 1987, p.xi.

65   Eric Hobsbawm, *The Age of Extremes*, Abacus, London, 1994, p.3.

67-8   E.P. Thompson, "The Peculiarities of the English", *The Poverty of Theory*, Merlin Press, London, p.61.

Marion Maddox

Amanda Lohrey's *Voting for Jesus* provides a welcome introduction to those jointly embarrassing and increasingly colliding topics, religion and politics. As I write, politicians of all parties are co-hosting a forum in Parliament House to highlight Australia's Christian heritage. The former deputy prime minister John Anderson reportedly told the invitation-only crowd of 300 church and political figures that secularism had "gone too far" and Christianity needed to reassert itself as the "dominant national belief system".

Lohrey's engaging account helps open a response. Indeed, it often reads like a conversation-starter, or notes for a class discussion. Her text is interpolated with questions, which often remain unanswered. Why does Phil and Chris Pringle's Oxford Falls Christian City Church lack the profile of Brian and Bobbie Houston's Hillsong, despite their being virtual clones? And why are Oxford Falls' congregations smaller? How valid is the social gospel, and how far can it be prosecuted as a strategy for the Centre Left?

The biggest question of all is not spelled out, although implied all the way through: why, given the secularism of mainstream Australian society that Lohrey so convincingly portrays, has the Howard government bothered? Why so many Hillsong visits, so much symbolic legislation aimed at little beyond religious button-pressing, such prolific appeals to Christian sentiment (from the Treasurer's "return-to-the-Ten-Commandments" prescription for Australia's social ills to the Prime Minister's annual pleas for a more Christian Christmas)? And why the harsher, not merely symbolic moves, such as efforts to entrench the "traditional" family (the anti-gay-marriage amendment to the *Marriage Act*, overturning the ACT's civil unions legislation) and the contracting-out of formerly government activities (such as welfare and job placement) to church agencies?

Lohrey paints churches as scolding the government for human rights and social justice failings, while cynically pitching for a conservative "moral" agenda and bigger slice of government money. But, even if true, that hardly explains the extraordinary effort on the government's side to courting what is, everyone agrees, at most a small, and politically divided, Christian vote.

Rather, much of the government's strategy with respect to churches has been an attempt to counter the kind of damage inflicted by mainline church criticism of Liberal policies – especially on land rights, multiculturalism and Hewson's GST – before Howard's 1995 return to the leadership.

The strategy involved three strands. First, senior ministers repeatedly berated church leaders who criticised government policy for being out of their depth (Costello), "partisan" (Howard) or "hogging the limelight" (Downer).

The second strand involved cultivating an alternative Christian public voice, associated with the capitalism-friendly "prosperity gospel" and emphasising personal salvation rather than social justice. The important spin-off of this American borrowing has been the provision of a conservative language of vaguely Christian public morality – not too overtly doctrinal to alienate the secular mainstream, but bland-sounding "family values" rhetoric, whose religious inflections were still deniable. Its target was not conservative Christian voters (of whom Australia has very few – and those few were always going to vote mainly for the Coalition anyway) but the secular mainstream. Religiously inflected language of "personal responsibility", "traditional values", "traditional marriage", "Judaeo-Christian values" and so on implied a moral rubber stamp for policies which otherwise might sound off-puttingly unfair (such as punitive "breaching" rules for the unemployed, or tax arrangements which disadvantage the worst-off, or benefit arrangements which favour high-income families over those where both parents need to work, or increasing government funding to private schools at the expense of state schools).

The third strand required taming the welfare and social justice agencies who had previously provided much of the policy critique which, as Howard so frankly admitted, had been particularly damaging "to our side of politics". The contracts for welfare delivery which Lohrey sees as the result of a successful church assault on the public purse were in fact initiated by the government, and often strongly resisted by church agencies themselves. Indeed, the contracts often included "no criticism" clauses, penalising the agencies concerned for speaking out even in their area of expertise.

While few had anticipated such an extraordinary clampdown on free speech, church agencies in the late 1990s knew well that the tendering system offered them a Faustian compact. I sat on the policy and ethics committee of one large church welfare agency through the period when such contracts were being introduced, and witnessed soul-searching debates about which was worse: to allow the organisation to risk being co-opted into what was, even then, clearly a cynical move, or to see welfare erode further. If they didn't take up the contracts, someone else would; but, with public sector welfare being whittled away, church agencies were major repositories of the skill, experience and collective memory vital to helping the most vulnerable people.

Church agencies' ambivalence has recently been further underscored by St Vincent de Paul's decision in April 2006 to refuse contracts for case-managing people breached by Centrelink, for fear that accepting them would imply endorsement of the harsh breaching policy (Vinnies still helps the people, but declines the government's shilling).

Lohrey rightly points out that religion is not easily quarantined from politics, and any attempt to keep it out (as some political philosophers and commentators have suggested) would in any case be highly undemocratic. But religion's effects in public life can also be potentially undemocratic. She helpfully draws attention to some of the dangers, and provides many starters for conversations about ways of keeping public life as democratic as possible.

So little used are Australians to looking at religion and politics that both the main currents and complex eddies are easy to miss. We need as many voices, and questions, as possible.

Marion Maddox

Edmund Campion

Two episodes stand out in Amanda Lohrey's *Quarterly Essay*: her encounters with evangelical Christian youths at the beginning and end of the essay. Both pieces of writing are alert, agile, swift and exemplary in their objectivity. She records what these young people say, without authorial interference or editorial comment. It makes one hope that she will pursue these encounters and give Australia a much-needed account of what, for instance, Hillsong is all about.

The Hillsong youngsters she interviews are in the middle of their teen years, so they cannot yet vote. Accordingly, her questions to them are non-political: questions about sex before marriage, God, the Bible, Jesus, salvation ... There's not much about politics in the first ten pages. Politics come in the following pages, which are a useful survey of recent newspaper stories (useful because not everyone reads the newspapers).

Like Marion Maddox in *God Under Howard*, Amanda Lohrey explores the emergence of a coalition between evangelicals and the hard political Right. She notices that this line-up crosses denominational divides, a novelty in our history. The sectarianism of past years has evaporated, as new sectarians find new targets, such as the Muslims. Today when an historian tries to tell young people that Catholics and Protestants were once at each others' throats, they find this incomprehensible. Yet the Reformation once impacted on our politics, as well as just about everything else. Beverley Kingston's *A History of New South Wales* is valuable in the space it gives to Catholic involvement in the ALP. As Graham Freudenberg, historian of NSW Labor, put it last year: "The early success of the Australian Labor Party owed a lot more to Cardinal Moran at St Mary's Cathedral, Sydney, than to Karl Marx at the British Museum, London." In 1949 Matthew Beovich, archbishop of Adelaide, wrote in his diary: "My strong opinion so far as *party politics* is concerned: the Church does not take sides, but she assumes a benevolent neutrality to that side which is most concerned with the workers and the poor, and the less privileged of the citizens."

In the light of this history, the appearance of Catholics on the front and back benches of the federal government is somewhat problematic. It would be improper to doubt their bona fides – Tony Abbott, for instance, has written lucidly of his sense of vocation as a politician and he has compared his present "calling" to a call to the religious life (cf. *Church and Civil Society*, Adelaide, 2004). Nevertheless, some elements of traditional Christian social teaching are hard to find on that side of politics. For instance, the growing insistence on centralism seems to contradict the principle of subsidiarity, which Pope Pius XI promoted to stop big entities taking over the function of grassroots bodies. Similarly, the common Catholic motto "a preferential option for the poor" is not one often employed on government benches. And what would a traditional Catholic activist make of the demonisation of asylum seekers? Puzzling.

Edmund Campion

Peter Jensen

It's hard to quarrel with experience, so I hesitate to take on many of the claims made in Amanda's Lohrey's testimony-based essay. She explains the reasons for this approach in her introduction and the desire to hear ordinary believers rather than religious leaders. Indeed, there is a moving, if brief, testimony to her own experience at the end of the essay.

On the other hand, experience has its limitations. I can tell you all about a foreign place, but my perceptions are limited, especially if I do not speak the language, have little understanding of its history and am at the mercy of what the locals do and don't tell me. Indeed it may well be that I have spoken to a very unrepresentative group.

Lohrey, of course, writes for us about the experiences of others, especially the young and the disaffected. But at a deeper level her essay is the voice of an experience that she herself is having – the experience of grappling with a religious world-view. She has made a journey to an (apparently) unfamiliar place and is reporting what she has found. She is not unsympathetic to the inhabitants, but she is not going to dwell in their midst long enough to go native herself. The dogmatic trappings make that impossible.

An experiential approach is not necessarily unreflective. On the contrary, it is quite possible to be properly critical of your own experiences, bringing intellect and experience together in a fruitful way. But it does not give primacy to the intellect in the way that other philosophies do. I think this explains my initial disappointment with Lohrey's essay. My expectations were misplaced, through anticipating a discussion of history, theology and politics and an engagement with some of the really serious thinkers in these areas before turning to contemporary Australian practice. This was not to be.

On the other hand, there are limitations to testimony, experience and personal reflection. This is especially evident in the section of the essay where

Lohrey is laying the theoretical foundation of what follows, the section entitled "Imago Dei". Even if you adopt an experience-based method, there is need to demonstrate a grasp of the subject at hand, despite the fact that it may be called "dogma". Here Lohrey courageously gives her own version of what Christianity is about and what it means. But is that enough to illumine a subject as profound as "Christianity and Politics in Australia"?

The problem is that for those seeking an intellectually credible account, her rendition of Christianity under the heading of *imago dei* bristles with difficulties. If we are dealing here simply with Lohrey's testimony, I suppose we may leave her assertions – her own "dogmas" – without comment. But surely this part of the essay should contain an intellectual engagement with the realities of Christianity, rather than Lohrey's unsympathetic account of her version of Christianity.

For example, Lohrey makes creative use of the theological concept of *imago dei*, applying it at once to representations of the divine in religion. "Jesus", she writes, "may or may not be the one true God, but he is not the only *imago dei* that the human imagination has given birth to. The Hindu pantheon alone has over 3,000 different god-images."

Now it is true that Jesus is referred to in terms of image in the New Testament. But in actual Christian theology, of whatever stripe, the *imago dei* is first and foremost God's gift to every human being, for we are all created in the image of God. Whether there are 3,000 Hindu deities I do not know, but that there are at the moment something like 5 billion persons on earth who are in the image of God, I do know. In short, it begins life in the Bible as an anthropological term. Later it is applied to Christ, but in ways which rely on the fundamental "image of God" language of Genesis.

That this illustrates a tendency towards a serious distortion of basic Christianity is at once apparent. Her versions of the fundamental Christian ideas are adrift. Is it true that "In Christian cultures there is a gap between God as a form or force beyond human understanding and God as accessible totem, and this is a gap that the Jesus figure has the potential richly to fulfil"? The audacity of leaving out the Old Testament conception of God, with its intimate portrayal of the covenant-making Lord who created and saved and spoke words of promise – a view which in any account is the bedrock of the Christian doctrine – is astonishing. The God of Christianity is built on this. He is no incomprehensible "form or force". He is the loving Father.

Or, what of the reference to "the grubby world of the material"? The Christian account of the material world is not that it is "grubby" but that it is "good, very good!" (to quote God's words in Genesis). Indeed, both the incarnation and the resurrection of the body are testimony to that positive attitude to the world of the material.

Or, what of the sentence, "About the historical Jesus we know nothing for certain, other than that he was a young Jew who managed to aggravate the Romans sufficiently to crucify him"? If we wished to be truly sceptical, we could also doubt that he existed, or that his real name was Jesus, or that he was young, or that he was crucified. All these "certainties" have been questioned. I am not sure on what intellectual grounds Lohrey stopped being sceptical where she did. But, then, what is the point of being as reductive as this?

If we judge things by the appropriate historical measure, we can, with great confidence, say much, much more about Jesus, not least about his teaching on the kingdom of God. Given the importance of this one biblical phrase in discussions of politics, should not Lohrey have paused to examine it? It is especially relevant to the discussion of church and state, and would have had explanatory power for the material which follows. Here is a startling omission, based on an impressionistic account of the current state of play in the study of the historical Jesus.

Or, what of her reference (following Lakoff) to "a judgmental and punitive Judaic God" who sends Jesus as a Saviour from sins? Apart from this offensive and inaccurate reference to the "Judaic God", why has she not mentioned that the model of Jesus as Saviour is what inspires the Christian affirmation that "God is love", full of mercy and compassion, and hence a great deal of Christian public action?

To express such idiosyncratic views of the fundamental Christian doctrines of God, of the human person, of the creation and of redemption, suggests a problem of understanding at a crucial point in the essay. Can it be that such an astute observer does not grapple with the intellectual side of the Christian faith because she believes that it either does not exist, or that it has been thoroughly discredited, or that no one from her point of view can take it at all seriously, indeed is not bound to try to understand it? I would be interested to hear what she has to say about this. We know that she has read at least one recent account of Jesus, and that may have led her to say more about his kingdom, for example.

Which brings me to the Boyer Lectures. It is an honour to be included in the Lohrey discussion and I hesitate to respond. But the editor has invited me to contribute, and so my response is largely limited to her interaction with my lectures. Let me say at once that far from being disappointed about the reception and effect of the lectures, I have been gratified. For example, I am informed that the first print run of the book has now sold out and that CD sales have been three times as many as usual for the Boyers.

Part of the reason for this is that there is in fact a great deal more of Jesus in the national psyche than some commentators seem to realise. That they rarely think or talk about him is deemed proof positive that others do not either. I am concerned that a knowledge of Jesus is declining, but I am far from admitting that he has become an absentee.

Now I am the first to agree that in a series of lectures such as these there are limitations to the scholarly apparatus which can be deployed. No doubt the same applies to *Quarterly Essay*. I was initially concerned to read that the lectures rely on "several logical and rhetorical sleights of hand", but reassured when the sole example cited is so clearly a misunderstanding of what I actually said.

I asked, "What do you do with Jesus? How do you explain his sheer historical importance while denying his divinity?" As a reference to my text will quickly verify, this is part of my discussion of a problem which confronted nineteenth-century European culture. The assumption of the centrality of Jesus was in force, while his divinity was being questioned. The two things are not logically connected (as Lohrey correctly discerns), but they certainly were historically (as she fails to acknowledge), and we are dealing here with a major revolution in human thought. I am sorry that she did not pick up my discussion on the kingdom of God in Jesus, rather than this marginal historical point.

She responds to my suggestion that we could do worse than once again appeal to the biblical history of Israel as a national *mythos* by stoutly defending the Anzac story as a replacement. To do so she says, first, that "only a minority of Australians declare themselves to be Christians"; secondly, that "There is more widespread and collective and individual feeling about young Australians who lost their lives in war than about the crucified Christ"; thirdly, that my attempt to move Jesus back into the "national debate about our lives" is odd, given my enthusiastic acceptance of the secular state enshrined in the Constitution. All this leaves me "stranded in a kind of no man's land of his own making".

Well, opinions differ. I understand that at the last census a strong majority of people still identified themselves as Christian, a fact if true which actually reverses Lohrey's argument. On the second assertion, I can only beg to disagree – and to make the point that the Anzac story was long ago incorporated into the Christian story at various levels. War graves are still marked by a cross (see George Mosse, *Fallen Soldiers*, Oxford University Press, 1990). Christ and his cross still animate the lives of millions in our country at various levels, every day and not just one day of the year. On the third point, Lohrey's enthusiasm for politics clouds her vision. I am happy to live in the secular state; indeed, my theology helps lead to a secular state. But the state is not the nation. The nation itself has never been secular, despite the hopes of so many.

However inadequately, the Boyer Lectures are saying that the kingdom of God remains alive and well. It does not support any call to a theocracy. It does not create unanimity on the political issues of the day. But it has let loose powerful spiritual forces in the world, which can be used for good, not least when the individual politician consults his or her conscience in the light of the teaching of Jesus. This, rather than alarms about such ephemera as the Christian Right, is a matter worth consideration.

Peter Jensen

Paul Collins

When I first saw this *Quarterly Essay* in the National Library Bookshop, I thought impatiently, "What the hell does Amanda Lohrey know about Christianity?" The unequivocal answer is "A damn sight more than I expected!" I found the essay insightful, provocative and at times quite brilliant. The thing is, Lohrey, unlike so many other writers on religion in Australia, takes theology seriously. With no religious sensitivity themselves, most commentators treat religion purely as a sociological phenomenon. Amanda, your Catholic education didn't let you down! For me the essay provoked comment rather than criticism, so what I have to say here is more in the spirit of continuing discussion than disagreement. While the essay is about the political influence of the new evangelical and fundamentalist outfits like Hillsong, Lohrey says correctly that the traditional churches, particularly the Catholics, are still the main game.

However, some of the mainstream churches are facing a crisis. The Anglican and Uniting churches have had catastrophic collapses in membership since the 1950s. For instance, in the 1954 census Anglicans constituted 37.9 per cent of the population. In 2001 they were down to 20.6 per cent, with a very low practice rate. The Uniting Church suffered an even greater decline. Catholics, meanwhile, have climbed from 22.9 per cent in 1954 to 26.6 per cent in 2001. Nevertheless, some think that within a generation Catholics will face the same kind of crisis. A decline in practice has already occurred: a reasonably accurate national count showed that only about 15.3 per cent of Catholics attended Sunday Mass in 2001, and there is evidence that this proportion has dropped even further over the last five years.

Personally, I am doubtful that the predicted crisis in Catholicism will occur. I think it depends a lot on the effectiveness of Catholic schools in forming a "Catholic imagination" in students. We all have a kind of pre-conscious filter, formed by family and education, through which each of us views the world.

One of the best explanations of this comes from Anglican theologian Graeme Garrett. He says that Catholics, unlike Protestants, still self-identify as Catholics even when they have given up practising their faith, "because they don't seem to be held so much by ideas as by something more poetic and symbolic, something sacramental". He defines this as "a cradling and embracing way of thinking, willing and being that you learn not so much with your head but through other people who already have it, and who mediate it to you via nurturing and formation". At its best Catholicism is community-oriented rather than individualistic. It's a bit like Judaism, really. This is why there are so many "cultural" Catholics around, people who are no longer convinced by Catholic doctrine and are critical of the institutional church, but are still held by a deeper religious feeling that comes to them more by imagination than by reason.

Unfortunately, Lohrey does not examine these issues but goes off on a tangent about church finances. Certainly the mainstream churches need to be held more stringently accountable for the use of public funds, but we need some context here. The Catholic Church educates 19 per cent of primary and 21 per cent of all secondary students in Australia (totalling 665,000) in just over 1,700 schools, employing 42,500 teachers and over 15,700 non-teaching staff. It runs the largest non-government health and aged-care system in the country, employing around 30,000 people and representing about 13 per cent of the whole sector; it supports the largest voluntary charity, the St Vincent de Paul Society, with 44,000 members and volunteers; it has a sizeable overseas aid budget through Caritas; and, if you put all the Church's work together, it is probably the largest employer in Australia after the federal government.

These statistics provide context. And they show that Hillsong and fundamentalists of all types constitute a very minor part of the religious landscape, with a little more than 1 per cent of the population involved. Lohrey is right to emphasise that the kind of fundamentalism represented by these people is a subcultural phenomenon. One might also be tempted to add that it is sub-Christian. It will never represent more than 15 per cent of explicitly religious people.

Running right through Lohrey's essay is an emphasis on the centrality of Jesus – from the "cool girls" and Hillsong to Archbishop Peter Jensen. And an important aspect of this is Jesus without the church, although I was rather gobsmacked when I read Peter Jensen saying, "I find it hard to like the institutional organisation [of the church]. And I don't really think of myself as a religious person." This from a man who organised and continuously struggled for two decades to get control of Sydney Anglicanism, by far the wealthiest Anglican diocese in the world and one of its most hidebound.

In the essay there is a particularly good discussion of Jesus as the *imago dei*. Lohrey shows that Jesus cut loose from religion and theology ultimately becomes the projection of the idealised self, "a screen on which we project our concerns". In the "Jesus. All About life" advertisements, Jesus is represented as a good bloke, a mate, a chap who fulfils my needs. The ads are almost Arian. Arius (c.250–c.336) was a priest in Alexandria who maintained that Jesus was not divine but rather a man especially created by God, a kind of fourth-century superman. This view was widely popular and led to many conversions in subsequent centuries simply because it was easier for ordinary people to understand than complex Trinitarian distinctions. It is amusing to think that the Bible Society who commissioned the ads might well be perpetrating a kind of 21st-century Arianism!

This "Jesus fulfills you" style of rhetoric is not only tacky but also ignores the fact that Jesus was a first-century Jew, with all that that implied culturally. Contra Lohrey, we actually do know a lot about the historical Jesus and his times. This knowledge acts as a check on the tendency to reinvent Jesus according to our own image and culture. Certainly it is interesting to see the Reformation debate about nature, grace and freedom being revisited by Lohrey's cool girls. "You get saved basically by just accepting Jesus," even though you remain sinful and evil in the best Protestant *sola fides* (faith alone) tradition. Essentially this is a limitation on human freedom, as Erasmus and the Council of Trent (1545–63) clearly realised. The Catholics had a more optimistic view: they held that Christ's death and resurrection not only led to the forgiveness of sin but also to the internal transformation of the human person into someone better.

The Protestant view also creates big problems for the salvation of the virtuous non-Christian. Catholicism moved decisively at the Second Vatican Council (1962–65) to recognise unequivocally the salvation of the unbeliever. Recently there has been a reaction against this, which can be traced back to the then Joseph Ratzinger, now Pope Benedict XVI: that is, a reaction against too much accommodation with the other great religious traditions, particularly as stated in the letter *Dominus Jesus*. Much of this reflects Ratzinger's Euro-centrism rather than a need for Catholicism to retreat from the broader ecumenism. But it does point up the unresolved problem of the Christian belief in salvation through Christ alone, and what is on offer for those for whom Jesus is a peripheral figure or is entirely unknown.

While a semi-Arian image of Jesus might appeal to the cool girls and to secular ad men as a way to a problematic, remote God, my experience is the opposite. Jesus is the problem, not God. Snobbish though it may seem, it is my observation that most reasonably educated people are more likely to have experienced some form of spirituality and transcendence in their lives – through the environment, great art, music, the goodness of others, love and, dare I say it, the church – than they are to be attracted to Jesus as a figure of salvation. I suspect it is the immature, the less educated but materially successful, or the merely technically educated, who are taken in by the Hillsong phenomenon or by fundamentalist evangelicals.

I agree that the churches desperately need a whole new approach to our culture, but rather than rushing in with Jesus as the answer, they ought to begin by listening carefully to contemporary questions. And the most fundamental questions that I hear constellate around the relationship between the experience of transcendence, the search for meaning and an ethic to guide life, and the relationship of all of this to God. Many thoughtful, perceptive people have already experienced something that takes them out of and beyond themselves, but they find it hard to relate that to the image they have of the Christian God as a kind of a harsh, angry old man in the sky. Many still have to get beyond their psychological hang-ups and childish projections.

A couple of other points: first, Cardinal George Pell is not the "head" of the Catholic Church in Australia. He is the Archbishop of Sydney and his authority ceases at the borders of that archdiocese, which actually has a smaller Catholic population than the archdioceses of Melbourne and Brisbane.

And, talking of George Pell: Lohrey is understandably astonished by the Cardinal's call to rethink the meaning of democracy. He says he wants a "normative democracy", which Lohrey interprets as "Christian democracy" or even a theocracy. Actually, Pell's views are simply a rehash of those of John Paul II. At the core of Pope Wojtyla's moral philosophy was the "personalistic ethic". He maintained that all genuine relationships are governed by this. He set this up in opposition to what he called the "utilitarian ethic", by which he meant a moral approach whereby we *use* others. In the Vatican II *Declaration on Religious Liberty* (1965), Catholicism broke away from the old notion of the state supporting and enforcing the established church to declare that religious coercion be abandoned and people be conscientiously free to choose their own religion and, by implication, morality. John Paul (and Pell) believe in freedom and democracy, but think that liberty is essentially a freedom to do what the natural law and the church as its guardian lay down as right. This is different from the emphasis in the *Declaration on Religious Liberty*.

Pope Wojtyla was concerned that contemporary Western democracy had become intrinsically intertwined with moral relativism in its search for a minimally divisive ethic. He argued that personal freedom and democratic structures need the guidance of the unchangeable moral law, which will determine what is acceptable civil law and what is not. Civil laws that allow euthanasia, contraception, divorce, gay unions or abortion, actions which are contrary to the intrinsic moral make-up of humankind, are symptomatic of ethical relativism and must be rejected. He believed that the pope and the bishops were the trustees and guardians of the universal moral law. What John Paul really wanted was a kind of ecclesiastically guided Catholic commonwealth in which church, culture and state worked together, justly and equitably, for the social and spiritual good of the community. How this differs from a benign theocracy is hard to see. Despite the Pope's expectations, not even post-communist Poland was willing to accept this approach.

Above all, it is hard to see how John Paul's idea would work in a pluralistic society. He, of course, had never experienced genuine democracy. Pell has, so his stance is doubly incomprehensible. He confuses pluralism and a kind of militant secularism that attempts to exclude God and the spiritual from civic life. Pluralistic democracy in the Anglo-American world simply acts – as Lohrey correctly says – "as a neutral referee between competing belief systems".

Finally, there is no evidence whatsoever that Christianity is dying out faster in Australia than anywhere else in the world, despite Benedict XVI's off-the-cuff comment to a small group of priests during his vacation last year in the Italian Alps. God knows where he picked up that idea. Hasn't he seen what's happening in France, Portugal or the UK, or even at home in Germany over the last four decades? Probably what happened was that an Australian bishop hoping to score some ecclesiastical brownie points told him this during his *ad limina* visit (bishops have to report to Rome every five years). It might even have been George Pell. Whoever it was, the Pope's statement is clearly not an example of infallibility at work!

Paul Collins

Tim Costello

What a treat it was to read *Voting for Jesus*! Amanda Lohrey provides a rich analysis of the intersection of Christianity and politics at the 2004 election: full of humanity, sincerity and salience.

While the subtitle of the essay suggests an analysis of Christianity and politics in Australia, what we are treated to is more of an excursus on certain conservative Christian influences on Australian politics. There is, of course, much more to Christianity and politics in Australia than that, and I am sure that Amanda, along with her readers, does not assume that these are the only representative groups within the Christian faith.

The stories that book-end Lohrey's analysis provide a better clue to her overall thesis. The views represented are those of young people who share few political beliefs and who are not easily categorised. The three girls interviewed at the beginning are members of a Pentecostal youth group and are quite different from the more Reformed members of a Sydney University Evangelical Union (EU). For an essay on Christianity *and* politics, these are curious cameos. Were the girls from the youth group there to dispel one image of those who attend the Hillsong church? And did the students from the EU serve to show that not all conservative Christians adore Hillsong and vote Family First? The personal stories Amanda recounts bring a richness to the essay, but they don't sit that easily with the promised "politics" in the title.

Let's examine the political side of the equation for a moment. In Australia and most other Western countries, increased church attendance pretty much predisposes one to vote for the conservative side of politics. In Lohrey's essay we don't get any direct analysis of why the ostensible followers of the unquestionably radical Jesus can seem so wedded to the status quo, but we do get some disturbing vignettes: the brilliant philosophy lecturer loses his faith in the Master because his present-day disciples are unwilling, metaphorically, to overturn the tables in the temple; the former head of the NSW Law Reform Commission, a Uniting Church member himself, concludes that the churches are the inveterate enemies of any social justice-based reform (a claim I seriously question); and the Family First Party appears wedded to giving preferences to the Coalition no matter how much the Labor Party promises to address the churches' justice issues.

The 2004 election gets talked up as the most significant intersection of religion and politics since The Split. But in truth most Christians voted pretty much as they usually do. Figures from the Australian Electoral Study (AES) suggest in fact a slight increase from 2001 – from 28 per cent to 29 per cent – in weekly churchgoers voting Labor. This appears to have come mostly from Catholic weekly churchgoers, 36 per cent of whom voted Labor (up from 31 per cent in 2001, but still way down from the 1993 high of 51 per cent). But in the 2004 election the Coalition *also* saw a rise in the overall churchgoing vote in the House of Representatives. This tells us that there was a substantial rise in votes by one of the Protestant denominations to make up for the Catholics who left the Coalition in 2004.

But which one? The Labor Party also increased its vote among Anglican and Uniting Church weekly churchgoers from 2001 to 2004. However, in the same period there was a rise in the vote for the Coalition in those weekly attendees who ticked "Other Christian" in the AES survey (other than Catholic, Anglican, Uniting Church, Presbyterian and Orthodox): a rise from 49 per cent in 2001 to 58 per cent in 2004, and a drop in the vote for Labor from 25 per cent to 16 per cent.

Which still leaves 26 per cent of the Other Christian voters unaccounted for. Twenty-one of the 26 per cent ticked the "Other" political party category, and their votes seem to have gone mostly to the Family First Party, which analysts claim emerged from the Pentecostal Assemblies of God Church. Family First picked up 210,567 first preference votes in the House of Representatives and, according to Haydon Manning, senior lecturer in the School of Political and International Studies at Flinders University, 9 per cent of those votes came from Catholics, 39 per cent from Protestants and 43 per cent from "Other Christians". (Of all Family First voters, 57 per cent were weekly churchgoers and around 70 per cent attended at least once per month.)

Which all means that there is indeed a conservative Christian nexus of Coalition and Family First voters, one that blossomed at the last federal election and bloomed amid the Pentecostal and independent charismatic churches. So why did this part of the Christian community rediscover its voice within civil society?

Was it a reaction against what was seen as "leftist" tendencies in the recognised voices of the church leadership? Or was it a response to a political and cultural impasse, such as the moral aridity of economic rationalism, disappointment at the loss of any genuine third way, or the enveloping atmosphere of pessimism in this time of fear?

Perhaps churches, like unions, have over the past few decades been losing "paid-up" members while gaining constituents – people who are not formal affiliates but who look to them to take the lead in representing a counter-cultural set of values. The larger picture of the Christian faith and politics in Australia has traditional churches still articulating deeply held values that resonate with a wide audience and which offer refreshment to people worn down by the secular, individualist/materialist mainstream culture ... even if they are not putting bums on seats in the way they used to. There are many in society who will never darken the doors of a church building but would deeply mourn the loss if the churches ceased to speak out on behalf of refugees, indigenous Australians, problem gamblers and the poor here and overseas. On many issues, such as the government's decision to join the Iraq War in 2003, the mainstream church representatives were united in a strong protest even though this was ultimately, and deftly, deflected.

The trend with the large megachurches, however, runs counter to the experience of most mainstream denominations. The growing attendance of young people at megachurches is both burgeoning and impressive. For these young people it too is a counter-cultural choice. The "cool girls" of Lohrey's essay are idealistic, enthusiastic and looking for something that answers to their social and spiritual needs. The Pentecostal context provides a lively and entertaining program that competes with the *Big Brother* vision of life and replaces the need for the culturally condoned pressures of night-clubbing, heavy drinking and random pick-ups. It is a Christian youth subculture that emphasises personal responsibility and fulfilling your God-given potential. It resonates naturally with conservative values of personal morality, domestic law and order, and free-market opportunity. But it also teaches the central Christian message of putting others' needs before one's own – so that these churchgoers are still open to the justice issues addressed by the mainstream churches. This is a natural consequence of the Good Samaritan teaching, and that these young people know this story is saying something, given that this is now effectively the first generation that has not had any Sunday School.

The question is whether these religious and lifestyle choices translate into life-long convictions and attendant moral and perhaps political choices. And here we should look beyond mere voting choices to what this means for civil society. The Make Poverty History movement both here and overseas has been effective in increasing aid commitments and debt relief because it has included faith groups across the religious spectrum. Indeed, in the UK an external analysis described church and faith groups as "unsung heroes of the year … vital to the success of 2005". There as here, faith groups have been mobilised into lobbying MPs, attending events and performing other campaign activities.

The broader impact of these changes will need longer term research to uncover. Lohrey's suggestion is that for many it is a stage they grow out of. I'm not so sure.

I was deeply moved by Lohrey's conclusion that went beyond dogma to shared experience and shared mystery. It is at the heart of many a search for a transcendent vision or, as Manning Clark put it, the search for "the image of Christ" in the culture.

Tim Costello

Andrew Dunstall

When I heard that Amanda Lohrey's *Quarterly Essay* would be an analysis of Christians in Australian politics, I was immediately interested. As a committed Christian in my mid-twenties, I am always intrigued when Christianity comes before the public eye. Perceptive, accurate and positive reporting on Christians in the Australian media is hard to come by, but yet again, unfortunately, I was disappointed. What I would like to take issue with is Lohrey's uncritical use of the word "fundamentalist", and her avoidance, indeed rejection, of any kind of thoughtful and reflective Christian thought.

The latter first: the best part of Lohrey's essay were the "book-ends" consisting of interviews with young Christians. It was touching and insightful to hear real stories. However, in both instances, when the conversation reached a point of reasonably rigorous debate, or something of lasting profundity was said, Lohrey retreated and hid behind her age, refusing to engage with the ideas and fobbing off her interviewees' comments with "How likely is it that their faith will endure?" or "I couldn't help wondering how this issue might translate for them in later life." This certainly doesn't help to promote a critical political engagement among the young, and smacks of paternalism.

Lohrey doesn't seem to have any interest in constructing a rigorous dialogue concerning the place of religion in public life. It would seem that she would prefer that the Christians remain silent and keep out of public life. But this has greater implications than simply for Christians. It doesn't take a genius to point out that the Liberal Party does not own God, or Jesus, or Christianity. But for Lohrey not to offer an alternative mode for talking of these things in public life means that it is equally impossible for Buddhists, Muslims and other religions to be able to speak meaningfully in public about their beliefs. Muslims, in particular, surely need to be allowed to defend themselves in our current paranoid society.

If we could construct a discourse on these things apart from the stereotype of "right-wing" and "fundamentalist"– without trivialising the beliefs of different religions by intimating that they are all essentially the same – there would be an effective avenue for critiquing the Liberal Party's abuse of values politics, and for not isolating and suppressing an important part of life for many Australians.

This, of course, brings me to the term "fundamentalist". *Voting for Jesus* uses the word twenty-three times. The problem is, Lohrey never actually defines the word. In fact, I have rarely come across a definition elsewhere either. Is it just a vibe that we recognise? In the essay, the word refers to, among other things, a broad collection of individuals, a "brand" of faith, a type of politics, "models" of Jesus (that happen to be the traditional description of Jesus from the Bible), the dogs at the call of Howard's whistle, cults like the Exclusive Brethren, right-wing MPs, a groundswell in society, anti-abortion campaigners, a kind of "mafia" and, strangely enough, Mel Gibson.

The manner in which Lohrey employs the word is entirely uncritical – as it is in most journalism. Unfortunately, this use creates a Christian bogeyman that menaces the media and good secular humanists everywhere. As Philip Nitschke said in an opinion piece in the *Sydney Morning Herald* on 20 July 2006, referencing Lohrey's essay, there is "a fundamentalist, all-denomination Christian lobby" that is shaking the ground in politics. It is no longer Reds under beds – it is Christians. Boo!

"Fundamentalist" has become so elastic a term that it can now encompass whatever we dislike about a political opponent. I have heard two Anglican ministers, who believe almost the exact same doctrine, labelled "moderate" and "fundamentalist" respectively, largely based on their debating style; one being good at "spinning" a debate, the other being more combative. The word is used as a knock-down punch, silencing discussion. But the perceived ideological weight that goes along with the word – and yes, Lohrey is coming from an ideological position, for we all hold to *fundamentals* of some stripe or another – is unjust, and it should be abhorred by journalists everywhere.

It is clear that a more rigorous debate concerning church and state is needed. We cannot do this while the spectre of the word "fundamentalist" hangs over us. Lohrey's simplistic understanding of church and state – that politicians should leave their convictions at home – is not productive. Nor does it suggest a way forward for Labor. There is much Christian thinking that would be categorised as left-leaning. Unfortunately, until now, there has been little effort to engage with Christians, or anybody else for that matter, by the Left. There are many aspects to choose from: a passion for refugees, for the poor and underprivileged, for the environment, for education and health – all of these have their place in the Christian ethos. Holding neo-liberal economics or right-wing politics as *a fundamental* is *not* the same as holding Christian beliefs or values. In fact, neo-liberal dogma is exceedingly opposed to the idea of family that most Christians hold to, as the recent WorkChoices legislation has demonstrated.

Although Amanda Lohrey had many good points to make, the fact that she does not provide an open and inclusive manner for talking about these issues – her dismissal of Kevin Rudd's efforts are again a telling point – surely drives home the point that we are still failing to come up with ideas in order to confront the moralising values politics that is the current status quo at a federal level. When interviewing the EU students, Lohrey mentions they show signs of "thinking for themselves". What a pity she hasn't herself done this. All she has done has used dog-whistle politics ("fundamentalist" is the whistle) to whistle up all the old lefties.

Andrew Dunstall

Bill James

There is a contradiction at the heart of Amanda Lohrey's essay. On the one hand, she is seriously concerned about the influence of conservative Christians on Australian politics. On the other, she is aware that conservative Christians represent a tiny proportion of the population and can be safely ignored not only by their fellow citizens, but also by politicians when it suits them. The size of Australia's evangelical community (including Pentecostals) is difficult to estimate because evangelicals are both intra-denominational and cross-denominational, but it is probably about 3 per cent, the same as that of the UK.

The important point to grasp is that Australia, like the rest of the West, is smack-bang in the middle of a secularist surge which began about forty years ago. For a long time it was the accepted wisdom among historians that secularism had been steadily progressing ever since the Enlightenment and the Industrial Revolution of the eighteenth century, but the publication of Callum Brown's The Death of Christian Britain (2001) demonstrated that secularism only really took hold in the 1960s. The result has been a succession of cultural upheavals, of which gay marriage is only the most recent.

As part of this trend, vocations and church attendance in the Roman Catholic communion, and membership of the mainstream Protestant denominations, are plummeting. To use a Melbourneism, they are in more shit than a Werribee duck. Eminent theologian Wolfhart Pannenberg has predicted that theologically liberal churches will have ceased to exist before the end of the century.

It is not correct to conclude that we are therefore living in the post-Christian era. On any Sunday morning there are more Anglicans in church in Nigeria than in the UK, USA and Australia combined. South Korea is second only to the US as a sender of evangelical missionaries. The church is large (nobody really knows how big) and growing in China despite fifty-seven years of communist opposition, while in traditionally Roman Catholic Latin America vast numbers of the poor are exercising a preferential option for Pentecostalism.

What we are witnessing in the West are the death throes, after seventeen centuries, of the partnership of church and state birthed by Constantine in the early fourth century. Conservative Christianity, both Roman Catholic and evangelical Protestant, will continue to exist, but will never again exercise the cultural and political clout which it enjoyed for so long. The irrevocable trajectory is toward a pre-Constantinian Christianity which is small, independent, counter-cultural, committed and entirely voluntarist.

In legislative and political terms, it is rapidly ceasing to matter what evangelicals think about issues such as abortion and homosexuality. The reality is that we already have *de facto* abortion on demand, and that is not going to change. A majority of the population want accessible abortion, and politicians know it. *Vox populi* might not be *vox Dei*, but it is the sure guide to electoral success. Even in the United States, where evangelicalism is much stronger than here, thirty-three years of determined effort, and a succession of conservative presidents, have not been able to overturn Roe v. Wade.

Homosexual marriage has been blocked for now, but it will pass eventually. It is all a matter of demography. Both here and in America, the generations which grew up with Christian cultural mores, if not a personal faith, are dying off. Moral Majority, which started off with a bang a quarter of a century ago, is now in disarray. Its leadership was devastated by the widespread indifference toward Bill Clinton's infidelities. In a previous era he would have faced universal opprobrium, resigned in disgrace and remained a permanent electoral liability, but as a result of the new ethical climate it is generally acknowledged that he would have won a third term had he been able to stand.

In Australia, the Pentecostal population has exploded for two or three decades, but its growth rate is now slowing down. This is because its catchment of former Sunday school and church members from the mainline denominations is drying up. Of the converts to conservative Christianity, a handful are absolute pagans, but most come from the (rapidly diminishing) ranks of those with a modicum of theological literacy. The election of Steve Fielding, as Amanda Lohrey demonstrates, was the result of a psephological snafu by ALP strategists who misdirected preferences, not a groundswell of support from a massive new constituency of politically aware Pentecostalists out there in the electorate.

Within the conservative churches, the issues of abortion and homosexuality are not the preoccupations which outsiders such as Lohrey imagine them to be. At ten years of age I experienced an evangelical conversion as a result of the 1959 Billy Graham crusade, and for the subsequent forty-seven years I have belonged to evangelical churches here and overseas. During that time I have never heard a single sermon on either issue, and I could count on one hand the number of times I have heard them referred to in passing from the pulpit. One of the reasons for this reticence is pastoral; in any congregation there is likely to be at least one woman who has had an abortion, and at least one person who battles gay inclinations, and there is no point in homiletically exacerbating their difficulties. Another reason is the disappearance through chronological attrition of the pre-babyboomers' "moral exceptionalism", which abominated homosexuality as the ultimate transgression, a sin in a class of its own. Today's evangelicals and Pentecostals are more likely to treat gays in the same way they treat adherents of other religions – as wrong, but not uniquely depraved.

The situation in the United States is not all that different. Evangelicals there, as everywhere, object to both homosexual practices and the killing of millions of unborn children. However, they are not fairly represented in the media by the incessant harping on the handful of abortion clinics blown up by pro-lifers over the last thirty-three years, or by the stock television footage of the anti-gay protester from Central Casting with his ten-gallon hat, stars-and-stripes tie and a placard which says "Fags will burn in hell." The magazine *Christianity Today*, which is the voice of mainstream American evangelicalism, sometimes runs features and editorials on homosexuality and abortion. While uncompromising on principles, they invariably emphasise understanding, communication and sensitivity to suffering.

Amanda Lohrey's dissection of the Hillsong phenomenon – its slickness, glibness, consumerism, anti-intellectualism, shallow theology, emphasis on good looks and "power of positive thinking" psychology – is spot-on, but then, such features do not require any particular profundity of insight to discern. They hit you in the eye. As she herself points out, similar criticism of Hillsong's "health and wealth" heresy comes from other evangelicals and Pentecostals.

It would appear that despite her worries over some of the forms in which it is manifested, Lohrey is not opposed to Christian involvement in politics per se. Her criticism of the mainline Protestant denominations, which largely share her political views, is very muted, and pretty much restricted to their education policy. She makes much of alleged "dog whistles" to conservative Christian voters on the part of the Coalition, but she heartily signals (more of a foghorn than a dog whistle) her own partisan preferences, and appears to imply that she would not object to Christian politicians if they toed the correct policy line, i.e. if they were not "neo-liberal", "fundamentalist" and "right-wing". Her own opinions on issues such as free-market economics and IR legislation are of course "moderate" and "progressive". Some Christians would agree with her. Christians of every political complexion try to co-opt Jesus for their agendas, but so too do agnostics and atheists. He is claimed just as possessively by the Left as by the non-Left, in both the religious and secular realms. Not just Christians in general, but also evangelicals in particular, vote right across the spectrum. I know of one evangelical who is not only a member of, but a candidate for, the Greens. Would Lohrey have bothered to write an essay called *Voting For Jesus* if she believed that all or most Christians voted Green – or Democrat or Labor?

Lohrey is confidently censorious in her assessment of conservative Christianity's faults, but it is not clear, in this relativist postmodern era, from where she derives the absolute value system on the basis of which she passes judgment. She is dismissive of Christian claims that religion is essential for morality, and in naive, old-fashioned Enlightenment style she privileges the primacy of the "moral reasoning" of the "individual conscience". This raises two issues. First, what happens when another "individual conscience" comes up with something with which her "individual conscience" violently disagrees? Who or what is the arbiter? Secondly, where do our ideas of the good come from? None of us is the mythical "autonomous individual" worshipped by modernity, who creates his or her worldview *ex nihilo*. All of our ideas are derived from the ambient culture, and since the society which incubated the thinking of all of us was largely Christian in its ideals, this leads to the spectacle of secularists using inherited Christian categories to deconstruct Christianity.

The most worrying portion of the essay is Lohrey's employment of George Lakoff's assertion that the God of historic, credal Christianity is a punitive father-figure. It is not the jejune, stale pop-Freudianism which is the problem here, but the sinister echo of past attempts to exploit psychiatry to stifle unpopular opinions. At the same time as the Soviet Union was incarcerating and forcibly "treating" dissidents in mental institutions, those in the West who objected to communism, on the grounds that it was a dictatorial ideology which killed millions of people, were told that they were *really* suffering from a pathology which caused anti-communism, namely "authoritarian personality", a concept with about as much scientific validity as phlogiston.

"I wants to make your flesh creep," said the fat boy in Dickens's *Pickwick Papers*. Amanda Lohrey shares a similar ambition, in the pursuit of which she even invokes the t-word, theocracy. It just ain't going to happen. It is a straw man, or (to use the adjective which describes the Jesus propagated by heretics who taught that he was only an incorporeal phantasm) a docetic man.

Bill James

Angela Shanahan

I read the latest issue of *Quarterly Essay* because I have written myself about the importance of the rise in religion in public life, what Neuhaus calls the right of religion to be heard in the marketplace. Imagine my dismay when, aside from the factual errors and slanders (like bringing up a mysterious connection between John Brogden's political demise, Opus Dei and David Clarke – who is not in Opus Dei?!), I saw Amanda Lohrey portray a new Christian alliance as an intolerant Christian conspiracy. Why? Because Christians are organised and, much to the chagrin of Lohrey and a generation of baby-boomers who lost their faith, young people and some older powerful people are listening.

I spoke at the big meeting at Parliament House for the constitutional amendment banning homosexual marriage. It was an astonishing grass-roots response, and indeed a heartening ecumenical experience. The evangelicals simply have the organisational ability that Catholics used to have. So what? And as for the agenda itself, I don't think that being against something like homosexual marriage is at all intolerant; rather, it is simply an affirmation of the status quo, where marriage is the legal protection of the natural family. We have that in common with non-Christian societies the world over.

The same goes for things like pornography and abortion, issues which Lohrey, with the boring predictability of the post-Christian feminist, reframes as about women or tolerance. But the real crime that the new Christian push commits in Lohrey's eyes is that it simply will not accept that reframing, particularly of the basic concept upon which all human rights actually hinge, the right to life. The preciousness of human life and the dignity of the human person are valid Christian and non-Christian human concerns.

As for Cardinal Pell's view, he merely tried to make the point that when a democratic society abandons the idea of the sanctity of human life in the name of secularism, then maybe we are indeed falling into the dictatorship of the secular humanists ... a dictatorship that Lohrey obviously believes should allow for the presence of a lot of empty rights talk in the marketplace in the name of pluralism, but not of God talk in the name of the same democratic virtue.

Angela Shanahan

Tamas Pataki

There is much that is agreeable in Amanda Lohrey's consideration of an increasingly worrisome subject. To be sure, her handling of religion was rather too gentle in our current circumstances, and for a moment I was even tempted by her mollifying assurances to hope that talk of a Christian revival in Australia was mostly just talk; that a true fundamentalist groundswell would be sure to generate a salutary reaction; and that "people in the community will go about their moral adjudications as they always have, on the basis of liberal humanist values without need of instruction from the Christian Right."

Reflection soon moderated hope. As Lohrey herself points out, even if mainstream religious worship in Australia is in decline, the political influence of the religious, especially of that active miscellany passing as fundamentalist, is disproportionate to their numbers. Moreover, it is hard to see why Australia should remain immune to the religious, especially fundamentalist, contagion sweeping other parts of the world. Liberal or secular humanism is a relatively green shoot, and the atheism often associated with it has never had much large-scale traction. Historically, the resting state of much of humankind has been religious conviction: supernaturalism of one form or another, supported by ignorance, both inevitable and self-willed, by bad argument, and by wish-fulfilling thinking and superstition.

The major religions are more than wishful constructions, of course; they are vast assemblies of metaphysical dogma, institutions, ritual, historically refined ethical teaching, and so on, spreading well beyond their wishful foundations. Some of their ethical teaching, institutions and charitable activities are exceedingly admirable. But it is, I think, a fact, and a sad one, that their appeal to the majority of their votaries rests principally on claims about the properties and dispensations of supernatural persons, in this life and the next. Without this delusive appeal they probably would collapse. That they have not, and that they are not likely to, but, on the contrary, that they will in all likelihood flourish in the immediate future, is testament to the evergreening of wishful thinking and self-delusion in the human breast.

Most religions provide conceptions of idealised, powerful and protective supernatural figures with whom worshippers can continue dependent, oftentimes narcissistic, (pseudo)relationships whose prototypes emerged in infancy. That fact has a multitude of malign, and some benign and gratifying, consequences. Several of these are clearly illustrated in Lohrey's interviews with her young fundamentalists. They could not be more explicit: the relationship with Jesus, "loving Jesus", letting Him "enter their lives", is the salvation issue. Having a special relationship (frequently it is an identification) with a supernatural, omnipotent figure is comforting and gratifying in many respects. Being one of the Elect destines you for Heaven. Consigning non-believers to hell, or converting them – fashioning converts into one's own image – are also gratifying, though not of the best sides of human nature. The special relationship provides unconscious assurance that the good, de-sexualised parent is still available, loves unconditionally, will rescue one from one's own lust and knows everything worth knowing. On the face of it, Jesus ("God in a form we can cope with") is a perfect, unthreatening and asexual ideal. At a deeper level, the young dying God is charged (as his various predecessors probably have been since neolithic times) with eroticism, and a frisson is detectable in the conversation of some of Lohrey's subjects. The "awesome" idea of the young God's sacrifice for humankind has a variety of wish-fulfilling aspects. The "cells" formed by the young Hillsong people and their larger church community provide a group identity which enables them to share in the group's achievements and thus diminishes envy and sustains self-esteem. It also creates another outlet for aggression, through group assertion. Skye's joke that they were "terrorists for Jesus" probably expresses an accurate unconscious understanding of one function of her religious associations.

These are some of the relatively benign features of religious identity, but more baleful features also emerge in the interviews. The fundamentalist acceptance of the inerrancy of Scripture (indicating a frightening incapacity to reason); the hostility to out-groups evidenced in their naif confidence that even decent infidels will burn in hell ("much as it sucks") and the devaluation of everything Muslim; the fear of sex; the need to subordinate and control women; and the hatred and fear of homosexuality – these features are conspicuous in the descriptions of authoritarian and prejudiced personality in the social psychology literature since the middle of the last century and are, of course, largely definitive of religious, social conservatism today.

Young people haven't had much time to sort out their concepts, but in reflective conversation they usually are generous. In relation to damnation, sex and the role of women, however, Lohrey's young fundamentalists appear to be callous and thoughtless. Lohrey is moved to wonder several times why, in particular, issues concerning homosexuality and women – abortion, reproduction, ordination – and to a lesser degree "Law and Order", agitate fundamentalists of all denominations and religions more than war, poverty (even their own), plague or global warming. She recognises that these attitudes are linked and have psychological, not just dogmatic sources, but her attempts at psycho-social explanation fall far short.

Lohrey endorses a story received from George Lakoff, the gist of which is this: there are two models of family structure which are reflected in social/political dispositions: the strict-father model (conservative) and the nurturant parent (Left or liberal). The former is based on the traditional family model of the Old Testament and its teachings. The world is represented as a scary place and children are born bad and disobedient. A strict and powerful father is required to protect and punish them and teach them right from wrong. External discipline creates internal discipline. Dependency and weakness are bad. Women must be submissive. Thus, "pro-choice and gay-rights campaigns directly contest and undermine the traditional authoritarian father figure and in so doing constitute a threat to the conservative value system as a whole."

There is, of course, something in this and it is a pity that Lohrey does not develop it. The borrowing from psychoanalysis is obvious, but to make it work the model requires more psychoanalytic premises than Lohrey seems prepared to countenance. I've abridged her account, but even the longer version does not adequately explain why, to take the most emotion-fraught cases, the notion of women having "any kind of spiritual authority over men" (citing one of the young fundamentalists), abortion or homosexual relations, should open such depths of fear and loathing. (There are of course scriptural injunctions and, in the name of discouraging abortion, good arguments; but I don't believe for a moment that the embrace of scripture or argument account for the intensity of the fear and loathing.)

It is evident that the Bible cannot be the only source of the strict-father model, as Lohrey and Lakoff suppose, since the conception is found in cultures untouched by the Bible. Very likely, it is the actual experience of the child in the family, and not only in the patriarchal family: from the child's perspective, the interloping father may be a stern reality in even the mildest of family dispensations. But beneath the punitive, law-making, strict-father imago (a Freudian term adapted by Lohrey) which shapes one image of God, are imagos of the mother. She is generally comforting and loved, but a number of developmental lines converge to render her an unconsciously feared and despised being. On one such line, because she is so intensely longed for, sexually exciting and envied, but ultimately unpossessable, she arouses jealous and vengeful feelings, and consequently guilt and fear. The child comes eventually to fear his own contumacious and unsatisfiable desires, and may disown and project them onto the imago of mother. That creates the figure of a dangerous temptress who must be devalued and controlled. A flight to the strict-father may assist the child in weakening attachment to a "bad" mother and, by identification, to control his or her desires, but it is secondary. (Later, other "strong" figures may be sought, especially obsessive-paranoid types – like those unrelenting politicians who "stay the course" come what may – and divine, omnipotent ones.) Attraction to father is in part the result of a flight from the feared and devalued mother and the guilt and anxiety associated with her.

My suggestion is, then, that the fear of being subordinate to women, the need to control their seductive sexuality and reproduction, and the covertly punishing and vengeful attitudes towards women found in fundamentalist groups, arise primarily from the more or less generalised, defensive projection of the dangerous, temptress-mother imago.

Some of the hatred of gay men has a related provenance. The passive, receptive homosexual is seen as not unlike a woman, and so attracts the kind of sexism sketched above. St Augustine, recoiling from his youthful homosexuality, enjoined that no man should be permitted to use his body as a woman's. However, it is now well understood, and experimentally corroborated, that anti-homosexual attitudes stem most frequently from homophobes' guilt over their own homosexual impulses. In the male case, the homosexual phantasies occasioned by turning to the father may arouse guilt and shame and are frequently repudiated and projected. Many people try to suppress their homosexual impulses by combatting them in others. The patriarchal monotheisms offer another line of defense against homosexual desires. Some of the threatening consequences of turning to father can be mitigated by turning to the Father-in-heaven or his desexualised representative on Earth. Homo-erotic feeling and the need to communicate it are displaced, disguised and dispersed in socially sanctioned worship, adoration, prayer, episodes of controlled group hysteria, and so on. (I don't mean to suggest that that is *all* that goes on in religious practice.) Given that these religions can function to defend against guilt for homosexual impulses, it is unsurprising that so many people who are burdened by such guilt (certainly one aspect of original sin) should enter church hierarchies and institutions, and struggle with it there. Where there is an absence of supportive, latently homosexual institutions of the types perfected by the Catholic Church, for example, as in the fundamentalist Protestant denominations, homophobes may have to defend themselves against self-hatred more noisily by publicly despising or endeavouring to suppress their own impulses in others.

Lohrey is "shocked" and "baffled" by the hatred and "unforgiving view of homosexuals" that she encountered in her young fundamentalists. Adolescents are, of course, particularly vulnerable to prejudicial tendencies as they struggle to escape their early parental identifications and to fashion a consistent and stable identity. It is unfortunate when some of these tendencies receive enforcement from ancient texts and benighted religious teaching. In general, it is people who have not adequately resolved their infantile attachments, who live under the shadow of the imagos of the strict-father or the temptress-mother, who are drawn to religions that seem to validate their fears and prejudices. All gods will protect and console, on condition of submitting to them.

Tamas Pataki

VOTING FOR JESUS | Response to Correspondence

Amanda Lohrey

The relationship between religion and politics is one of great complexity and only so much can be addressed within the format of a *Quarterly Essay*. There are two kinds of essay one can write here: the specialist work that focuses in detail on a single issue within a field, and the generalist essay that attempts to give a broad overview. Clearly *Voting for Jesus* belongs to the latter category. I was responding to the need that I and others perceived for an essay on religion and politics that would canvass the field in broad terms and create an informed context in which the general reader could be alerted to recent developments, and from which base she or he could then seek to further their knowledge in any specific area that engaged their interest. Quite often in the past few years I have found myself remarking to friends and acquaintances on some news item or other, only to encounter the very common response of "How interesting, I didn't see that report" or "I meant to listen to that program and didn't get around to it." It seemed time for a recapitulation of recent trends and events that would bring the general reader up to date, and judging by the very positive response the essay has received it has been of value in achieving exactly that. Marion Maddox says that it reads like a conversation-starter or notes for a class discussion and I think she means to imply this is a deficiency, whereas I see it as the purpose of the essay, and the fact that it has been taken up by many book groups and some internet chat-sites attests to its usefulness in that regard.

There are of course important issues within the broader context that are worthy of specialist essays in their own right. I would be interested to read Professor Wayne Hudson on how we might go about developing a doctrine of religious citizenship in a globalised age, a subject he has addressed over many years in his distinguished career as a philosopher. There is also a timely essay to be written by a specialist in the field of political studies on what exactly it means for a politician to make a conscience vote within our current model of representative government.

Dr Peter Jensen objects to my opening emphasis, in the interviews with young people, on experience rather than the "primacy of the intellect". Giving precedence to the latter, of course, is characteristic of his particular brand of Protestantism and distinguishes it from the new Pentecostalism of, say, Hillsong. It was not my project to take theological sides in this division but rather to look at how some of the differences might translate into public intervention and political preference. Dr Jensen also feels that in my interviews with young Christians I am somewhat of a foreign traveller unable to interpret the depths of a foreign culture. This seems an odd description given that I share not only a common culture with these young people but that, as I make plain in the essay, I myself had a Christian upbringing, and not one of the token or "cultural" ones either but an intense and passionate engagement for which I remain grateful. It accounts perhaps for the sympathy I felt for the young people I interviewed, a sympathy that some militantly secularist readers regard as misplaced. Had I been interviewing young Muslims I might more accurately have fallen into the role of exotic tourist that Dr Jensen ascribes to me.

My interviews with young Christians have provoked a strong response, mostly favourable, but Dr Jensen not unreasonably suggests that they cannot be regarded as representative or objective in the way of an accurate statistical sample. This is true, and nor were they intended to stand in for a "typical" or statistical profile of an "average young Christian" (an impossible entity). Since they have provoked much discussion, and since Tim Costello in his correspondence questions their place in a political essay, I should perhaps say more about them here. They were conceived of by me, in a general sense, as exercises in the mapping of a sensibility, with a particular focus on the ways in which young Christians employ the faculty of moral reasoning. Collectively they represent a portrait of a certain sensibility at a given moment in time in a kind of show-not-tell mode, a mode that fiction writers have great faith in for its ability to create that empathy between reader and subject without which the "facts" of research are of limited value. An individual's sensibility may be characterised as resembling both an amoebic sponge and an arrowhead. The way we vote is the arrowhead, at a fixed point in time, while the sponge goes on absorbing new influences and shedding old ones. But voting, or any kind of political behaviour, arises out of a sensibility in flux, something that is a dynamic, evolving process, not a fixed pattern of rigid formation. I wanted to show this sensibility and its moral reasoning at work; its energy, its idealism, its internal strains and contradictions, its inherent beauty and dignity as a process of human thought and potential. If there is an "argument" in my essay, it is that this is a process we must respect and protect while allowing as full an expression of its many possible outcomes as is consonant with the principles of human rights that underwrite our liberal democratic system.

And while, as Tim Costello remarks, the Hillsong girls are not yet of voting age, they are on the brink and raring to go.

Dr Jensen is disappointed in my discussion of the *imago dei*. He feels that I have placed undue stress on the figure of Jesus and been neglectful of God the Father, and that this represents a serious over-simplification of Christian theology. I would have thought, however, that it was clear within the context of my essay that I am responding to the current emphasis on Jesus in many Christian congregations and promotional campaigns, especially in regard to mounting an appeal to young people. This may be a simplification or vulgarisation but it is not one of my making, and my research indicated that the emphasis on Jesus among young people is partly a non-response, or anti-response, to the Old Testament God the Father whom they find less appealing. In addition, I would point out that Dr Jensen's own Boyer Lectures play on this contemporary emphasis in their focus on Jesus, even down to the cover of the published lectures which features an image of Jesus wearing an iPod and headphones, a cover to which I assume Dr Jensen did not object.

Questions about the historical Jesus are for biblical scholars and textual analysts. I simply referred to the welter of contested material in this domain. To the interested observer it appears now to be commonly accepted that the Gospels themselves are the fiat of a committee and that other gospels, other teachings were overlooked. Protestant theologians differ radically on the question of, for example, the Resurrection. Catholics have found justification for the elevation of the spiritual status of Mary, while Protestants regard her as an ordinary if admirable woman. And so on. I do not "grapple with the intellectual side of the Christian faith" because it is not my purpose to mount an intellectual critique of Christianity as such. As I have said, and it seems keep having to repeat, I am not an atheist or militant secularist. I am surveying recent Christian interventions in Australian political life and their apparent foundation as laid claim to in public statements by religious leaders. The theological debates must be conducted by others. As for my discussion of Christianity and the Anzac myth, I feel it is inaccurate to say, as Dr Jensen claims, that I "stoutly defend" the myth. I merely refer to its enduring currency, and its emotional potency for young people who, in increasing numbers, make pilgrimages to the Dardanelles, and I compare this to Dr Jensen's argument in the Boyer Lectures that the Bible ought be reconsidered as the basis on which to found a mythos of nation. My point is that where strong Christian faith is waning, in terms of devout adherents, the argument for the latter is weak, and in any case it sits uneasily beside the Sydney Anglican church's otherwise strong support for the separation of church and state.

I am grateful to Paul Collins for his elucidation of the liberal Catholic position that arises out of Vatican II. Many non-Catholics revered John XXIII and greatly admire living spiritual leaders of the calibre of the former Bishop of Milan, Cardinal Carlo Martini. They do not perceive Cardinal Pell as espousing the same ethic. Contra Pell, the search for a "minimally divisive ethic" is not the road to a decadent "moral relativism" but the basis of social cohesion. That it is not equivalent to a degraded or weak moral position was evident in the case of the fatwa issued against the writer Salman Rushdie, when liberal democrats in the UK rose to his defence and were quite clear on the "absolutes" of their moral position and the limits of liberal tolerance toward those elements in minority cultures that are hostile to freedom of speech. That these same liberal democrats tended to be supporters of immigration and cultural diversity did not mean that they were not clear on the core values of their democracy. They were resolute in their defence and protection of Rushdie – himself an immigrant – sometimes at great personal cost. Those who attack "moral relativism" and multiculturalism seem to be wilfully blind to the fact that it is liberal secularists who are among the most strenuous defenders of, for example, the rights of women against oppressive cultural practices such as genital mutilation, enforced marriage and barring access to education. They oppose these practices on the basis of Enlightenment doctrines of human rights about which there is nothing "relative". They do in fact speak to an "unchangeable moral law", one largely compatible with Vatican II leadership but not with the conservative reaction away from Vatican II in today's Catholic Church. I respect the role of liberal Catholics within the Church in striving to keep the spirit of Vatican II alive and they, better than I, know the difficulty of this in the present climate.

I take Paul Collins' point about cultural Catholics and also the contribution of Catholic social agencies. He reads my writing on the public subsidy of church finances as a "tangent" from the main debate, but I wonder if he doesn't underestimate the wider social implications of the great increase in funding to nongovernment schools. It widens the gap between social classes and exacerbates the problems of the disadvantaged. Though I attended a church school, I have taught in government schools and participated in them as a parent. Over many years I've observed the scandalous decline in their funding and the wider ramifications of this. For many children who live in disadvantaged circumstances, their school is a frontline of moral and material support; the difference, as many social surveys indicate, between surviving and going under. Opinion polls in the UK reveal that the one highly regarded area of Labour policy under Tony Blair has been his government's efforts to improve public education, with some degree of success. If Australian government schools were given the same support, instead of being drained of resources in favour of an already affluent private sector, there might well be less need for those Catholic welfare agencies. This is but one area where it seems to me that Jesus' injunction to show kindness to strangers is applied only where there is a comfortable "surplus" left over after first attending to the churches' own self-interest.

Andrew Dunstall is one of those correspondents who seems to have missed the point of my interviews with young Christians. The students agreed to be interviewed on the basis that I was there to listen, and it would have been neither seemly nor productive for me to have monstered them in debate and taken advantage of their goodwill by engaging in point-scoring. Nor do I understand Dunstall's claim that I would prefer that Christians "remain silent and keep out of public life", since I make it clear that I think all religionists in a free country have a right to put their point of view in the public arena; to argue the case, that is, as opposed to imposing it on a dissenting majority. Others have commended the essay for upholding that right.

Dunstall makes several other misreadings of my essay. I am not dismissive of Kevin Rudd's efforts within the Labor Party and I commend his astuteness in pre-empting attempts to smear the ALP as anti-Christian. I also acknowledge that many Christians are "left-leaning" (see the reference to Andrew Hamilton and *Eureka Street*). I agree that a "rigorous dialogue concerning the place of religion in public life" is desirable and I would welcome an essay on this by the likes of Wayne Hudson, but this was not the purpose of my essay. To "do justice to Buddhists, Muslims and other religions" is to explore the notion of religious citizenship in the postmodern world, a large subject well beyond the scope of my canvassing of recent Christian lobbying in the local political sphere.

As for my use of the word "fundamentalist", in my research for the essay I discussed this at length with various people, but there wasn't space to canvass its various forms in an essay that was not about theology as such. I drew on the commonsense understanding of the term to mean literal interpretations of scripture that transcend historical time and place and are not open to debate. Of course, this does not prevent the development of many variants of fundamentalism –

many different-though-literal readings of scripture – but the essential, non-negotiable character of the fundamentalist reading obtains in all cases. Dunstall says that he has "rarely come across a definition [of the term] elsewhere either", so I recommend to him the Sir Robert Madgwick Memorial Lecture "Fundamentalism, Christianity and Religion" given by Professor Philip Almond at the University of New England on 7 April 2004. A transcript of this lecture can be found on the *Encounter* website of ABC Radio National.

Like Andrew Dunstall, Bill James appears to have read the essay he expected to read rather than the one that is there in the text. He attacks me as militantly secularist, a position I have gone out of my way to disavow in a number of places (see especially the "Coda"). James defends the many evangelicals who are liberal on issues of social justice, but underestimates their current frontline role in the culture wars and more especially the often cynical and opportunistic mobilisation of their political interventions by neo-liberals who are as happy to exploit evangelical moral conservatism as they are to ignore whatever commitment they may have to social justice (see Marion Maddox). He personally may not have heard many sermons preached from the pulpit on abortion and gay marriage, and the focus within the evangelical congregations on these issues may indeed be as low-key as he asserts, but the strident debates within the public sphere are there for all to see – increasingly so – and need not be enumerated again by me here.

Would I, James asks, "object to Christian politicians if they toed the correct policy line, i.e. if they were not 'neo-liberal', 'fundamentalist' and 'right-wing'"? The question of whether I would have written an essay if I believed that "all or most Christians voted Green – or Democrat or Labor" is a rhetorical question and a patently silly one. The same structural and moral questions in regard to the relationship of religion to politics would arise, whatever the voting trends. The answer here is that I object to those politicians, Christian or otherwise, who do not accept our current model of the liberal secular democratic state. It's their political and moral authoritarianism I object to, latent or manifest, not their metaphysics. But this, in James's view, is an Enlightenment morality that he describes as "naive" and "old-fashioned" – a bit of a giveaway, this – and he is censorious of my "privileging" of individual moral reasoning (privileging it, presumably, over scriptural and clerical authority). Who or what, he asks, is the "arbiter" when one individual's reasoning clashes with another? The answer to this, as I argue in my essay, is the liberal secular state, a state that, unlike any kind of theocracy, is *ipso facto* a constant work-in-progress. It's never perfect and we do not assert its infallibility, we negotiate its refinement. The basis on which we do this may be influenced by our Christian traditions, as James asserts, but is as much if not more so by Enlightenment and Utilitarian forms of rationalism. What is "privileged" here, as I say in my essay, is that all positions must be debated, defended and re-negotiated on the basis of reasoning, a reasoning which of course can never be free of cultural conditioning but which is not anchored in the diktats of scripture. The liberal secular state safeguards, indeed guarantees this *process* and its relationship to majority consensus. Thus in our society a Christian is free not to have an abortion – is not compelled or induced as in China – but so also is a non-Christian or a liberal Christian free to choose not to have a child. Clearly James is not happy with my espousal of the secular state as "arbiter", but he offers no alternative authority of his own, other than a vague gesture in the direction of "religion" as the basis of morality.

Then there is his somewhat shoddy elision on the subject of "psychiatry", where any attempt to examine the underlying psychology of a political position is equated to the Soviet Union's confinement of dissidents to lunatic asylums. Come off it, Mr James. The various psychological accounts of the human are explanatory models we are free to take or leave, as those who have shopped around for a good therapist can testify. They are not theologies, indeed are constantly in the process of modification and re-negotiation. The removal of homosexuality from the US's *Diagnostic and Statistical Manual of Mental Disorders* (DSM) is a case in point. George Lakoff is not, as it happens, a psychologist; he is a professor of linguistics, and his analysis is based on the use of language and how this relates to models of affect within particular cultures, models that are a given in a particular culture – strong fathers, nurturing mothers – not some spurious invention of his own. It's true that there are reductionist psychologists who see all religion as neurosis and God as a displacement of an idealised parent, but there are also psychologists who are Christians, Hindus, Buddhists and Muslims.

I have two things to say about Angela Shanahan's correspondence. David Clarke, the Liberal member in the NSW Legislative Council, is not, she asserts, a member of Opus Dei. In my essay I reference Stephen Crittenden's interview with Clarke on ABC Radio National's *The Religion Report* of May 2004 in which Clarke describes himself as a "co-operator" of Opus Dei. Secondly, Shanahan speaks of a "generation of baby-boomers who lost their faith". What evidence is there for this? There is much evidence to the contrary. The so-called New Age movement and the growth in Westerners who are Buddhists and adherents of forms of Eastern mysticism has been one of the generally acknowledged outcomes of the so-called cultural revolution of the '60s led by the baby-boomers.

That some of them may have lost their Christian faith does not equate to them having lost all interest in the spirit. The growth of Buddhism in Australia is a subject that would make for an interesting *Quarterly Essay* in its own right.

There has been a large volume of correspondence in response to *Voting to Jesus* and for reasons of space it has not been possible to publish all of it. I would like to make mention here of a very interesting letter from David Collis, who wrote about the "extent of the justice traditions at work in mainstream evangelical churches" and their work to, among other things, lobby for the cancellation of Third World debt (also referred to by Tim Costello). David is an active member of the Greens Party in Victoria and a former Greens candidate in the 2001 federal election. He argues that I have skimmed too lightly over the progressive Christian tradition and I think this is fair comment. David believes that we are witnessing the beginning of an important "Greens–Christian nexus" and whether or not this proves to be the case, he is one of those who happily scramble any tendencies others of us may have toward stereotyping in the field of religion and politics.

Amanda Lohrey

Edmund Campion is Emeritus Professor of History at the Catholic Institute of Sydney. He is the author of *Australian Catholics*, among other books.

Inga Clendinnen is a distinguished historian of the Spanish encounters with Aztec and Maya indians of sixteenth-century America. Her *Reading the Holocaust* was named a *New York Times* best book of the year and awarded the NSW Premier's General History Award in 1999. Clendinnen's ABC Boyer Lectures, *True Stories*, were published in 2000, as was her award-winning memoir, *Tiger's Eye*. In 2003 *Dancing With Strangers* attracted wide critical acclaim. Her latest book is *Agamemnon's Kiss: Selected Essays*.

Paul Collins is a broadcaster and writer. Among his books on Catholicism are *God's New Man: The Legacy of Pope John Paul II and the Election of Benedict XVI*, *Papal Power*, *Upon This Rock: The Popes and Their Changing Rome* and *Between The Rock and a Hard Place: Being Catholic Today*. His latest work is *Burn: The Epic Story of Bushfire in Australia*.

Tim Costello was ordained a Baptist minister in 1986 and is the former president of the Baptist Union of Australia. In 2004 he was appointed CEO of World Vision Australia. He is the author of three books: *Streets of Hope: Finding God in St Kilda*, *Tips from a Travelling Soul Searcher* and *Wanna Bet? Winners and Losers in Gambling's Luck Myth* (with Royce Millar).

Andrew Dunstall lives in Sydney and works in academic publishing.

Bill James is a former history teacher who has also lectured and tutored in church history. He has worked in India in a missions support role.

Peter Jensen is Archbishop of the Anglican Church, Diocese of Sydney, and Metropolitan of the Province of New South Wales. His ABC Boyer Lectures, *The Future of Jesus*, were published in 2005.

Amanda Lohrey is the author of *The Philosopher's Doll* and the award-winning *Camille's Bread*. She has published many essays on Australian political life, including the acclaimed *Quarterly Essay 8, Groundswell: The Rise of the Greens*, and two political novels, *The Morality of Gentlemen* and *The Reading Group*.

Marion Maddox is Reader in Religious Studies at Victoria University, Wellington. Her most recent book is *God Under Howard: The Rise of the Religious Right in Australian Politics* (2005).

Tamas Pataki is Honorary Senior Fellow and sometime lecturer in the Department of Philosophy, University of Melbourne. He is co-editor, with Michael Levine, of *Racism in Mind* (2004).

Angela Shanahan is a freelance journalist whose writing has appeared in the *Australian, Canberra Times, Telegraph, Age, Adelaide Review, Spectator* and *Quadrant*.

www.ingramcontent.com/pod-product-compliance
Lightning Source LLC
Chambersburg PA
CBHW080608090426
42735CB00017B/3364